· THE ·
LAWDOG
FILES

CASTALIA HOUSE

Fiction
Brings the Lightning by Peter Grant
Rocky Mountain Retribution by Peter Grant
The Missionaries by Owen Stanley
An Equation of Almost Infinite Complexity by J. Mulrooney

Non-Fiction
SJWs Always Lie by Vox Day
Cuckservative by John Red Eagle and Vox Day
Equality: The Impossible Quest by Martin van Creveld
A History of Strategy by Martin van Creveld
Compost Everything by David the Good
Grow or Die by David the Good

Military Science Fiction
Starship Liberator by David VanDyke and B. V. Larson
Battleship Indomitable by David VanDyke and B. V. Larson
The Eden Plague by David VanDyke
Reaper's Run by David VanDyke
Skull's Shadows by David VanDyke
There Will Be War Volumes I and II ed. Jerry Pournelle
Riding the Red Horse Volume 1 ed. Tom Kratman and Vox Day

Science Fiction
City Beyond Time by John C. Wright
Somewhither by John C. Wright
The End of the World as We Knew It by Nick Cole
CTRL-ALT REVOLT! by Nick Cole
Back From the Dead by Rolf Nelson
Victoria: A Novel of Fourth Generation War by Thomas Hobbes

Fantasy
The Green Knight's Squire by John C. Wright
Iron Chamber of Memory by John C. Wright
Summa Elvetica by Vox Day
A Throne of Bones by Vox Day
A Sea of Skulls by Vox Day

·THE·
LAWDOG
FILES

LAWDOG

CASTALIA HOUSE

The LawDog Files

LawDog

Published by Castalia House
Kouvola, Finland
www.castaliahouse.com

Editor: Vox Day
Cover: Steve Beaulieu

Contents

Dedicated to Rita.

I love you.

Foreword

When I approached LawDog about writing the foreword to this book, I told him I would consider it an honor, because I was a fan of his stuff twenty years ago. His response? "What? Twenty years... We're getting old."

Yep. That's like ten million years in Internet Time. I was a college student when I discovered this internet gun forum called *The Firing Line*. Because most of the posters thought of themselves as Serious People discussing Serious Business, it could get a little dour at time.

Until this one guy in Texas decided to introduce a little levity with some true life stories about the day-to-day adventurers of a peace officer in a small town.

When I got to the armadillo, I about got kicked out of the campus computer lab because of—and I quote—"disruptive laughter". Luckily, making people laugh is rewarding, so LawDog kept on telling us stories. Over the years there were more cases, more critters, and more weirdness.

I got to know LawDog, and he ended up being one of the people who inspired me to try and become an author myself. In fact, it was a Halloween joke thread that LawDog started, with gun nuts coming up with silly horror movie lines (because let's be honest, most horror movies would be over fast if they were about our people), but that helped me put together the basic idea behind my first novel.

The thing about good humor writers is that they don't just make you laugh, they make you think. *The LawDog Files* can get a little philosophical at times because these are basically the stories of an honorable guy doing challenging things to try and help folks, and then afterwards sharing the good bits to brighten someone's day.

I'm honored to call Dog a friend. I hope you readers get as much enjoyment out of these stories as I did.

Larry Correia
Yard Moose Mountain

Introduction

Hello, my name is LawDog. Thank you for buying this book.

What you are holding in your hands is the culmination of about a decade's worth of writing about a lifetime's worth of experiences. It is also the result of some fairly persistent nudging by various and sundry online folks, some gentle hints from my lady, and, last, but by no means least, a firm shove by some good friends. It is a collection of tales that I have written down for posterity and shared on my blog as well as some additional thoughts tacked on for good measure.

I generally tell two distinct kinds of stories: the first are of my law enforcement days as a small town deputy sheriff in Texas, and the second are of my childhood in Africa. This book consists of the law enforcement stories in Texas, during the closing years of the 20th century.

Enough blathering. On to the stories!

FILE 1

Armadillo Love

This is the first story I ever posted to the Internet.

Back in the late 90s I was a regular on the forums run by the old Rysher production company which was, at that time, running a show on TeeVee called Soldier of Fortune.

Mind you, at that time I didn't watch the show, but I did like the regulars at the Forum, amongst whom was a young lady who went by the nom de cyber of "psyche."

At times during the course of the Forum, the posts and debates got very serious—I'm talking complete and total Sense of Humor Failure—to the point where psyche finally posted a plea for a little more light-heartedness.

Prior to reading her post, I had been reminded of an embarrassing incident from earlier in my career, and I figured, "Hey, nothing's quite as funny as making fun of your own self," so I wrote a quick anecdote based on the incident and posted it.

And a small bit of Internet history was born.

In the late 1990s a lady in our fair city had gone on a date with a local fellow, and while the evening had been nice enough, the romantic connection seemed to just not have clicked for the lady in question, and she decided that they should just remain friends.

Now, apparently the phrase "let's just be friends" didn't quite sink in with the old boy, or perhaps he had a completely different definition of friend, than, well, everybody else, and he began parking his car across from her place of work and staring at her from it for hours at a time. He also began making a continual series of phone calls, the usual stalker stuff, all culminating in a panicked 911 call at 0300 hours when she woke up and found his face pressed up against the glass of her bedroom window.

He went to jail, and we had a quiet talk with a local justice of the peace, who issued a protective order for the lady in question.

This protective order seemed to work for a couple of days until she reported that the critter was now sneaking into her garage and moving stuff around.

The sheriff predictably went ballistic at this defiance of his directive and swore a mighty oath that Joe Critter was going to get sent off for a long time. However, in order to do that, it was felt that said critter needed to be caught in the act.

You know where this is going.

Since the Bugscuffle County Sheriff's Office had a grand total of four sworn officers, and three out of the four officers were married with children, it should come as no surprise to anyone that I, as the only unmarried and unentangled deputy, was tapped for this particular Special Duty.

Now, the young lady in question lived at the top of hill just outside the southwest city limit in a big old two-story house with an apricot orchard out back and shrubbery everywhere.

I showed up that evening, checked in with the lady, and wandered the grounds for a bit, trying to find the best spot from which to lay an ambush. The driveway was long and swept from the road up to the garage and was bordered on both sides by a pyracantha hedge. The yard was absolutely filled with bushes and plants of all varieties, and I figured that on a moonless night, the critter's best bet was to sneak straight up the driveway rather than risk tripping over a root and going head-first into a rose bush.

So, I found a nice little gap in the hedge near the house and figured on waiting until the critter was well within the "do not go within three city blocks" section of the protective order before dashing through the hedge and arresting him.

I bellied down under the tree, and I waited. And waited. And waited.

Along about 0100, an armadillo wandered up from the aforementioned apricot orchard behind the house, where he'd been feeding on fermenting apricots all night, and bounced off my foot.

I hear the gentle reader's question now: How did I know it was a he armadillo? Simple. The drunken little sot promptly, and aggressively, fell in love with my left boot.

sigh

He would sidle up to my boot, murmuring, "What's your sign, baby?" in armadillo-ese, and I would shove him away, whereupon he'd sleaze back in, crooning seductive armadillo love songs.

And so the evening went. I'd kick him across the lawn, he'd roll a not-inconsiderable distance, hiccup, and promptly oil his way back. About two hours later, I'd had it. I was just about to stand up and drop kick the Armoured Menace into the next state when I heard the crunch of feet tip-toeing up the gravel driveway. I froze, locking in on that gap in the hedge—I had a sneaking suspicion that the armadillo used my distraction to make it to third base—

and saw a shadow move in front of the gap. I took off like a shot, only to find out that some commie pinko liberal had somehow moved the gap in the hedge.

I also found out that *Pyracantha* is a Latin word that means "Deadly Demon Vampire Bush from Hell." I don't know who screamed louder: the armadillo, when his lady love disappeared; the stalker, when I grabbed a good handful of his shirt; or me, when I crashed into a brisket-high wall of finger-length thorns.

The lady of the house heard the triplicate scream, decided that the unthinkable has happened, dialed 911, and screamed, "That deputy is getting killed!"

sigh

Meanwhile, I'm half bent over the thorn bush, trying to hold on to a panicked stalker with my right hand and a walkie-talkie with my left hand. There is struggling, there is swearing, and somehow, in the middle of all this goodness I end up halfway over the hedge, upside down. I looked past Joe Critter down the road... and all I saw were lights.

Red lights, blue lights, yellow lights, white lights, flashing lights, strobe lights, wig-wags, you name it. All of them were rapidly coming up the road.

About that time, Joe Critter managed to twist loose. He hotfooted it down the road, leaving me with his shirt.

I got on the walkie-talkie, waited for a pause in the traffic from the SO, DPS, EMS, and game warden all demanding to know what had happened to me, and said, "I'm all right. Subject is a white male, no shirt. Northbound on foot."

It is possible, when viewed in retrospect, that in light of the circumstances, I may have lacked a little of my customary *sang froid*.

You see, the various deputies, firemen, EMTs, park rangers, security guards, DPS troopers and LEOs from all eight surrounding counties and towns heard my voice on the radio and thought: the 'Dog sounds panicked. The 'Dog don't ever panic! Therefore the 'Dog has obviously been shot/stabbed/gutted/burned/run over/abused/whathaveyou and is, no doubt, in immediate danger of expiring.

sigh

Anyone who hadn't already been coming to the party decided they had better show. Before long, Joe Critter was spotted halfway down the road and promptly became the subject of a multi-jurisdictional pig pile.

As for me, there I was, upside down and helpless in the grip of that fiendish hedge. And what did my friends, my brothers, my comrades-in-arms, my drinking buddies do to help me in my time of need? "Hey! Who's got a video camera?! We have GOT to get video of this!"

It took them thirty minutes to get me loose from that plant. I never did see that drunk armadillo again. Good thing, too.

FILE 2
The Good Shoot

My first story involving the Alcoholic Armadillo was a big enough hit amongst the denizens of the Rysher SOF Forum that I began to receive repeated requests for "More!"—repeated to the point of pestering. To take the pressure off of my poor email inbox, I began to write what became called "Psyche's Story For The Week."

I'm not sure how many of these little scribblings I wrote on that Forum—anywhere from a dozen to twenty-something—and I never really considered them important enough to save. The short-sightedness of this was rendered apparent when Rysher was bought, the forum archives were lost, and then the forum was gone. Along with everything I had written. Vanished. All gone.

Missing the camaraderie of the Rysher Forum, I wandered for a bit before I stumbled on to Rich Lucibella's TheFiringLine.com, joined, and before long I noticed someone was complaining about the lack of humor there.

Rather than posting the Armadillo Story, I recalled a later story involving Santa Claus, and since Psyche wasn't a member of TFL, I titled the anecdote "The LawDog Files."

I imagine that the choice of title probably had something to do with "The X Files," which was a wildly popular television show at the time, but I don't know. I never watched "The X Files."

A critter well known to us in our town twisted off one evening and decided to add Attempted Murder to his *curriculum vitae* by hitting his lady *du jour* in the head a couple of times with a hatchet. Not one to leave a job half done, he dragged her out to the lake, wired her up to a cinderblock, and shoved her off into the water. Wonder of wonders, she survived. Even bigger wonder, she came into town and filed charges on her homicidal boyfriend. I had been out on a date and wandered back into town about the time that the search was really getting wound up. I'd no sooner walked through the door of the office when the sheriff hit me with three conflicting orders on where to go, one of which would require asbestos underoos. I decided that going back home to change out of my date clothes would be counterproductive, so I was digging through my locker trying to find my spare set of armor when the call came in. One of our local merchants had spotted the critter climbing in the back window of an abandoned building used for storage. Since the other two deputies were on the far side of the county, the sheriff made a posse of me and a luckless Highway Patrol Trooper who had come in for a coffee refill, and we went tear-arsing off to Downtown Bugscuffle. The abandoned building in question had, at one time, been a fairly swanky department store positioned on the prize end of Main Street. However, in the intervening hundred years or so, the entire block had fallen into disuse and disrepair, leaving the once-grand old building standing all alone, used only for storing various and sundry stuff that needed storing by the locals.

For those of you who don't know how to search a large building with only three people, it's really quite simple. One officer, whom we'll call "the sheriff," stands on one corner watching the front of the building and the west side. The second officer, or "random DPS trooper," stands at the opposite corner of the building, watching the back of the building and the east side. The third officer, being the bravest and most handsome of the three, goes inside with the idea of flushing the critter out a window where he can be spotted by one of the other two and, hopefully, arrested.

Three guesses who got to go inside, and the first two don't count. Let me tell you, that place was darker than the Earl of Hell's waistcoat and stacked floor-to-ceiling with shelves. On those shelves were the collected knick-knacks of 20 years of Main Street stores. And not a lightbulb anywhere.

There I was, with a snubbie .357, a five-cell Maglight, and a Handi-Talkie, and only two hands. About the fourth time I tried to answer the sheriff's "Have you got him yet?" radio call while trying to cover a suspicious patch of darkness with the .357 and juggling the Mag-Lite, I stopped in the feeble light of the moon shining down through a hole in the ceiling to make a few adjustments.

I was occupied with trying to figure out which I needed more, the Mag-lite or the Handi-talkie, when the SOB decided to jump me. I'm here to tell you, folks, things went rodeo from there. He lunged out of a shadow and tried to grab for my throat, and me, reacting totally out of instinct, I whacked him a good one across the forehead with the Maglight.

Bulb, batteries, and assorted electronic parts arced gracefully into the darkness. The critter took one step back and jumped at me again.

Things were not looking good in Dogville.

I held the snubbie back with my right hand, trying to keep it away from the critter's grasp, and I tried to stiff-arm him away with my left when I stepped onto what was later found to be a D-cell battery from my Maglight.

Down I went. And the alleged aspiring axe murderer landed on top of me. Hoo boy. The gloves really came off then. We rolled around on the cold cement. I was hitting him in the head with the butt of my revolver and giving him elbow smashes to the jaw and brachial plexus, knee strikes, you name it, the whole enchilada. And he kept grabbing at my throat.

Finally, we rolled into a patch of moonlight, and I saw the bastard had a knife!

Folks, I hate knives. No, I really hate knives. He was on top of me, and he had to weigh three-hundred pounds, and that damn knife was coming down at me in slow motion at just about the same time the barrel of my snubbie rammed up under his chin.

I squeezed off two rounds.

The .357 magnum is a powerful round. Two of them, fired in quick succession, sufficed to blow the electronic brains and assorted stuffing of the Animatronic Life-Like Talking Santa Claus that formerly belonged to the local Thriftway halfway to Dodge City.

You don't want to know what a couple of .357 rounds will do to hydraulics.

sigh

So there I was, staring at the robotic Kris Kringle whom I had as-saulted, aggravated assaulted, and finally brutally murdered, when the sheriff and the trooper came crashing through the darkness looking for me.

The sheriff looked at me and the fallen Jolly Olde Elf and then began to stare fixedly at the ceiling while tugging his mustache.

Trooper Gary holstered his SIG, got out his pipe, looked around the crime scene, picked up a piece of flaming hat trim, and used it to light his pipe.

Trooper Gary: (puffing his pipe into life) "Obviously an assault candy cane. Bet it ain't registered."

Sheriff: "Dangerous things, assault canes."

Gary: "Obviously a good shoot, though." Puff, puff.

Sheriff: "Don't worry, boy. I'll call the marshals first thing in the morning."

LawDog: "Duh, puff-pant, huh?"

Sheriff: "Boy, there's gonna be several million kids after your hide come Christmas. Witness Protection Program is your only chance."

Smartass. That was the only time I have ever directed the Universal Peace Gesture at my fellow LEOs.

The critter was caught in New Mexico an hour later.

FILE 3

Pogonip

The story I wrote about the unfortunate death of Santa Claus at my hands had a sequel that I started writing at The Firing Line during my tenure there as a moderator. I say "started writing" because I had one of my frequent bouts of writer's block about halfway through the story, and it was several years before I was able to finish it and put it on my blog.

At the time I finished writing it, it was somewhat longer than my usual stories. I was a little worried that it was too long and that my readers would lose interest before getting to the end. I need not have worried, it turns out. This story is consistently mentioned as being one of my readers' favorites.

Show of paws here: how many people know what a *pogonip* is?

For the unwary, a *pogonip* is also called ice fog. It is basically a thick blanket of winter fog that freezes on contact with anything solid, forming a super-slick rime of ice up to several inches thick.

So now you know.

As penance for my brutal assassination of Santa Claus the year before, the sheriff had graciously allowed me to be volunteered to play the Jolly Olde Elf at the town Christmas pageant.

The suit was a wonder. Even wearing armor and a gun belt, I still disappeared in its deep red depths. This little problem was solved by the addition of several pillows from the trustee cell and three crumpled editions of the Sunday *Dallas Morning News*. The boots were actually overshoes, which velcroed quite nicely over my ropers, and the standard-issue beard was tossed in favor of something dug up by the chief dispatcher, who also did the wardrobe for the town theater group. She glued the beard to my face with some kind of clear adhesive, which she assured me would come off quite easily once the performance was over.

Lying heifer.

Anyhoo, I pulled on the supplied mittens, extracted my 15-year-old Shetland Sheepdog from under the dispatch desk, and drove my cruiser over to the Fire Department. The Sheltie was looking festive too, as the ladies in the office had given her a Christmas-themed sweater, put bows on her ears, and painted her toenails in sparkly red-and-green hues.

The night before, our area of West Texas had received one of these rare pogonips, which had rendered the entire area about as slick as a greased hockey rink, but I didn't realize how slick everything was until I wallowed out of the cruiser and slammed the door, which sent the cruiser sliding slowly about a foot left and into the gutter.

sigh

I rode the brand-new pumper truck over to the courthouse, did the "ho, ho, ho" thing, got my lap worn out, everyone exclaimed

over the Sheltie, and she suffered herself to have many, many
pictures taken with various personages. It was what anyone would
think of as a generally good day.

Not only that, but after the festivities, I discovered that the guys
at the Fire Department had been nice enough to pull my cruiser
out of the rain gutter. Twice.

I plunked the dog into the side seat, shoehorned myself behind
the wheel, and was gingerly inching my way home when, you
guessed it, the radio went off.

Burglary. In progress at one of the local churches.

I drove us over to the church, pulled up, and mindful of my
experience at the Fire Station, I got out of the cruiser, but I didn't
close the door.

Parked in front of the church was a pickup truck, its engine
still running. Across the street was a little old gentleman with an
absolutely huge mustache, holding a cordless phone and giving
me the old hairy eyeball.

I immediately assumed that the gentleman with the phone
was most probably the reporting party, so I started to wad-
dle across the street to get more information when I noticed
that someone else happened to be in the act of walking from
the front lawn of the church toward the pickup truck, and
this person also happened to be carrying one of the figurines
from the outdoor Nativity scene. This kind of struck me as
odd, so I hollered, "Sheriff's office, might I have a word with
you?"

The old boy heisting Joseph, or possibly one of the Wise Men,
immediately dropped the purloined porcelain and took off at a
high-speed shuffle in the direction of the pickup, thereby earning
himself the title of Person of Interest Number One.

Deciding that I really, really wanted to have a talk with that critter, I also kicked it into high gear heading for the truck.

He got there first, snagged the side mirror, pirouetted a couple of times, and went arse over tin cups onto the street.

However, he did this just before my feet abruptly kicked out from under me, and I went down as well. God bless the Dallas paper; I couldn't have been better padded if NASA had given it a try. I rolled over and started pushing myself to my feet when the critter righted himself, glanced over at me, and started a high-speed crawl slash bellyslide to the curb.

Once on the chapel yard, he found somewhat better traction, got to his feet, and abruptly took off at a dead sprint, me breathing down his neck. At the corner, he pulled a sneaky. Since he hadn't slowed to make a turn, I figured we were in for a full sprint down the block, but he put out an arm, grabbed the guyline for the telephone pole, and made an abrupt right turn. While this was, indeed, a good move, unfortunately, it dumped him on his fourth point of contact, and the critter slid a good ten yards down the street.

Not having benefit of the guyline, I turned right as well, only more like a battleship under full steam. I used the entire street and most of the yard across the street just to change direction, said extra room giving the aforementioned critter enough time to scramble to his feet and head back the way we came.

Apparently, I was still a bit too close for comfort because the critter ran past his pickup without even slowing down. This put him on a direct course for my cruiser, which, you may recall, still had the driver's-side door open.

I could almost see the 25-watt bulb light up over his head as he Got An Idea. Visions of dog-napped Shelties suddenly flashed across my mind's eye. Not to mention, of course, the thought of having a fully equipped sheriff's office cruiser stolen out from under my nose, but a man has his priorities.

Fortunately, the Sheltie chose that moment to daintily step into the driver's seat, fix the approaching critter with a gimlet eye, and utter a short, sharp "Ah'm wee, but Ah'm wickit" bark, thereby causing my critter to rethink his master plan and to lock up the brakes. This caused his legs to shoot out from under him, and he slid right under my cruiser, slick as a pin.

My last desperate grab for the Manger Bandit cost me my balance too, and I hit the ice, sliding along at full speed and scrabbling frantically at the ice because my concerns for a dog-napped pooch had suddenly been replaced by visions of my overloaded butt slamming into the cruiser and causing the whole enchilada to slide into the gutter.

By the grace of God, I narrowly missed my cruiser and slid into the gutter by my lonesome, which was not as bad as it sounds due to the extensive Santa padding. I spun about, and there was my critter, staring at me from under the cruiser about ten feet away.

"Right then, boyo," I snarled, "You're nicked. Let's go."

My critter blinked at me in utter incomprehension. "What?"

"You're under arrest. Let's go."

"No" sayeth the critter. Now it was my turn to blink in confusion. "What?" I wittily replied.

The critter turned over and got a couple of good handholds on the undercarriage of my cruiser. "Make me."

I pushed myself to my feet and stomped over to the cruiser. "You're under arrest." I gritted out through clenched teeth, "Now, get out from under there!"

"Work for it, fat man."

sigh

I was digging past various pillows and the lifestyle section of the *Dallas Morning News,* trying to lay a paw on my pepper spray, when my gaze happened to land upon… it.

There it was. In all its glory. Not twenty feet from the front bumper of my cruiser. A holdover from the heady frontier past of our fair city: a horse trough.

I happily—one might even go so far as to say joyously—ambled up to said horse trough, peered over the side, and saw it was absolutely chock-full of water, with only a three-inch-thick crust of ice over the top.

I made a few adjustments and then ambled back to the cruiser, watching my very own winter tidal wave flow down the gutter, and said, gently, "Time to come out from under the car."

He disagreed. "Don't you have an elf to play with?"

"It would really be in your best interest to come out."

"What are you going to do? Put coal in my sto–HOOOOoooo WHoooaaaa Ohohoho Haaaa! Haa! Huh-huh-huh!"

I tugged reflectively upon the beard. Yep. Between a combination of Panhandle winter wind and three quarts of glue, it was stuck but good. Under the cruiser, the yodeling briefly died down to a series of gasps and then crescendoed into a sudden soprano shriek that signaled, I surmised, the infiltration of polar water into the underwear area.

It was cold, apparently.

The impromptu yodelfest died down to noises strongly reminiscent of a rapid-fire castanets, so I cleared my throat reflectively and remarked, "There's hot coffee down at the jail, dry clothes, and a warm bunk."

"B-bb-b-bbb-bastard."

"Or I could come chip you loose when the cold snap breaks. I figure, what? This time next week?"

A dripping, shivering blue face appeared above the front quarter panel and stared accusingly up at me.

"I d-d-didn't kn-n-n-know S-santa Cl-Claus was such-such a s-s-sumbitch."

"Believe it. Into the back seat, Nanook. Let's go put you into a nice, warm cell."

FILE 4
Big Mama

This was the first of the stories involving the family of Big Mama, her four Amazonian daughters, and innumerable grand-offspring, and it was another tale that I'd been telling for years before finally writing it down at the Rysher site.

Oddly enough, it's the Big Mama stories that occasionally get me anonymously accused of racism online. I say "oddly enough" because I'm very careful to exclude any mention of race and am equally careful to write the dialogue in a vernacular that I consider to be "Southern Trash."

Come to think, it probably should be the Azikiwe stories that get me accused of racial bias, but so far, that hasn't happened. Ah, well.

Anyhoo, Big Mama was something else. I tooled up to arrest her one time for smacking one of her offspring in the snout with a steam iron. That woman proceeded to whip my butt with nothing more than a fly-swatter, a plastic Jesus, and a diaper bag.

———————

Big Mama was the matriarch of what passed for a crime family in our neck of the woods, and she came by the name honestly. I swear that woman was every bit of six foot four and an easy 400 pounds at her most athletic. While she wasn't exactly a criminal mastermind, what she lacked in quality, she more than made up for in quantity. And she never, ever, went quietly when arrested. While the Gentle Reader might consider this to be par for the course in rural law enforcement, I can only point out that in this particular case, we're talking about six feet, four inches, and four hundred pounds of berserk Mama Grizzly Bear.

One glorious day I was on duty when the word came in: Big Mama had Passed On.

We were in the middle of a Moment of Silence—"For this gift we have received, let us be truly grateful," murmured the sheriff—when the ambulance crew called, requesting help.

We had a problem. Hoo boy, did we have a problem. Big Mama had let her girlish figure slide a bit over the preceding several months to the point that the sheriff, two deputies, two paramedics, and the Bugscuffle Volunteer Fire Department couldn't even get her off the bed, forget putting her on the ambulance stretcher and its 300-pound weight limit.

After a couple of hours of creative swearing, we finally worked out a plan. Someone scooted over to the local monument company and borrowed its forklift and a spare pallet while the volunteer fire department got out the Jaws of Life and popped the exterior wall off of Big Mama's bedroom. Six of us rolled her onto the pallet, and then we raised the pallet and put it, and Big Mama, onto the hose bed of a fire truck. Voila!

Off we drove to the funeral home, where the director, bless his heart, had dug out a portable embalming outfit. I didn't even realize there was such a thing! Thanks to that, he was able to do the necessary deed on Big Mama in the garage.

Which, in retrospect, was probably responsible for what happened later.

The day of the funeral arrived. I had to be there because, true to form, four of Big Mama's nephews, cousins, and grandkids were in jail on various charges. My handcuffed, shackled, and leg-ironed charges and I showed up early, and I was impressed, let me tell you. Someone had somehow found a casket big enough, and Big Mama was laid out in her Sunday finest with a peaceful smile on her face.

This was shocking in and of itself. I had only ever seen Big Mama when she was fighting mad and cussing fit to make a sailor blush. Never saw her smile until she was gone. It looked downright unnatural.

Anyhoo, we were there early, and I was listening to the gossip, which was all based on whether Big Mama's youngest daughter would decide to show her face or not. Years earlier, Big Mama had attempted to rearrange this particular daughter's giblets with a set of pinking shears, and said daughter had wisely run off to California, vowing never to return.

Well, as it happened, she came back for the funeral. And I'm here to tell you that her performance there should have gotten her an Oscar. But I'm getting ahead of myself.

Four—count 'em, four—Baptist preachers got up behind the pulpit and lied their butts off about the Recently Deceased. Three different people got up to sing muzak versions of pop songs. The eulogy was a masterpiece; it bore no more resemblance to the Dearly Departed than a toady-frog resembles a polecat, but it sounded nice.

Then, finally, it was over. Almost. The family rose and walked past the casket to say their final farewells and to steal any jewelry left on the body, with the entire congregation looking on and sniffling. Last in line was Baby Daughter.

Like I said, her performance was a masterpiece. Baby Daughter had to be supported by two cousins in her time of grief. She was bravely fighting back tears, and as she tenderly touched the frozen features of Big Mama, she wailed, "Oh, Big Mama, why'd you leave us!?" And the two cousins gently tried to lead her away, but she turned back to the casket and blubbered, "But I can't leave her!"

Someone get that girl an Emmy.

This went on for about five minutes, until finally, Baby Daughter flung herself bodily across Big Mama and wailed, "Come back, Big Mama. Come back!"

And Big Mama did. Sort of. Well, actually, she kinda flopped a bit and made a noise like a humpback whale singing, as a glowing green ball appeared over the casket.

I remember thinking, "Aha! So that's what an air bubble in a corpse looks like. I always thought that was an urban myth. Fascinating."

Then, I noticed that I was the only person left in the church. Everyone else was sprinting down the hill, with the head preacher and my four leg-ironed prisoners leading the pack, I might add. It was at that moment that I noticed the glowing green ball was not an air bubble emitted from a corpse but rather the tritium insert in my front sight.

The next thing I noticed was that I was in a Weaver stance so solid that it took me about five minutes to bust my knees loose enough to sneak down the aisle to make sure Big Mama was still well and truly deceased.

I have been told there are rumors floating about that I actually poked the Dearly Departed with a stick during my subsequent examination. I deny the allegations entirely. I couldn't find a stick. So I stood at the Amen Pew and tossed flower arrangements at the old lady instead.

After all, you can't be too careful.

FILE 5

The Lovebirds

I was a little hesitant about posting this one as it pretty much has an R rating, and I thought my Gentle Readers wouldn't like the slightly racy elements. I shouldn't have worried about that, though, because my usual crop of readers loved this story.

However, this was written when my blog was starting to get really popular, and my readers were cross-posting everywhere. So this is the first story that netted me a vociferous avalanche of accusations of racism.

People who know me understand just how introverted I am, and those anonymous accusations almost caused me to shut down the blog.

Fortunately, about four hours into the flood of emails, I got angry over the sheer cheek of people who didn't know me and decided "Damn the torpedoes! I'm blogging! Just to irritate those idiots!"

Big Mama had four girls, and of the four, Opal was the most like her mama, both in temperament and body. In other words, one Opal would have easily made two of me, and I'm not exactly petite. Opal was as mean as her mama, and younger and fitter to boot.

And there I was, taking a leisurely patrol through the Bad Section of Town, when I noticed what appeared to be a nekkid man laying flat on his back in the middle of the dirt road, with Opal, fully clothed—thank you, God—sitting square upon his stomach, facing his feet. This, in and of itself, was enough to warrant further investigation, but the prostrate man was also beating upon Opal's broad back with his fists while screaming at the top of his lungs.

Kissing all thoughts of a tranquil evening goodbye, I checked my pepper spray, stepped out of the cruiser, and walked up to the lovebirds.

"Desmond," I greeted the gentleman, whose face was not unfamiliar to me. "Opal. What's on y'all's minds?"

"Go 'way, Mister Dawg," said Opal, without turning around, "This don't concern the law none."

"Oh, Sweet Jesus!" yelped Desmond, "Mister Dawg, you gotta do something!"

Well, Hell.

"Opal," I started to say as I eased around to where I could see her hands, "We need to talk... Holy *Mary!*" The anguish I heard in Desmond's voice was entirely understandable once I got far enough around the two to notice that Opal had Desmond's schnitzel in both of her ham-sized fists and was apparently trying to rip the old boy out by the roots.

I'm here to tell you, folks, walking up on that sort of thing without advance warning can make a feller get kind of wobble-legged around the knees.

"Opal!" I shouted, "You turn loose of that! Now!"

"No, Mister Dawg," said Opal, defiantly, "I feed him. I pay his bills. I keep gas in his car and clothes on his back. This belongs to me. He owes me."

You know, there are certain things the Academy just doesn't prepare you for. I repeated my demand.

"Opal, you turn loose of Desmond. Let him go to his mama's house, and then you come over to the car, and you talk to me."

"Okay, Mister Dawg. I don't care where Desmond goes."

Good, I thought, wondering just where the heck I had put the extra-large handcuffs.

"Desmond can go anywhere he feels the need. But *this* stays with me." So saying, Opal made motions somewhat reminiscent of opening a particularly stubborn ketchup bottle. Desmond's screams took on the silvery tone and dulcet quality of a World War II air raid siren.

"Opal," I interjected sternly, "Turn loose of Desmond, and let's talk about this."

"No!"

Well, so much for negotiation. I unlimbered my can of pepper spray, and then considered what a stiff dose of OC would do to Desmond's exposed anatomy. Okay, so maybe pepper spray was not my best option.

Out came the expandable baton. But what was I going to do with it, rap her knuckles? Damn.

Once more into the breach. I took a deep, steadying breath, eased up on Opal, threw one arm around her fire hydrant-sized neck, and promptly rammed the thumb on the other hand deep into the angle between her jaw and ear.

Things pretty much went pure rodeo from there. Opal screamed, she sunfished, she kicked, she twisted, and as a matter of fact, just about the only thing she *didn't* do was let go of Desmond's wedding tackle, even with me snarling, "Turn him loose, and I'll stop hurting you," into her ear and firmly twisting my thumb to emphasize my point.

Opal apparently forgot to attend the Pain Compliance Class where the smarmy little instructor confidently tells you that this technique will cause anybody to stop what they're doing and follow instructions because near as I could tell, not only did she not turn loose, she actually tightened the screws a good deal.

Leastways, that was the impression I got from Desmond.

Okay. Plan B. To hell with SOPs. I slid my arm across, snuggled in a good rear armbar choke, and hauled back for all I was worth.

sigh

Folks, now is the time to discuss "Leverage and Its Place in Law Enforcement." Specifically, exactly how much leverage is available to a deputy sheriff wearing leather-soled ropers, standing on pecan-sized gravel, such gravel being cunningly laid over a hard-packed *caliche* clay road.

Choke... sliiiiide... cuss.

Sliidddeee... choke... CUSS!

Swear... slide... swearswearswear... choke... cuss.

Somewhere in the middle of this, the sheriff's cruiser pulled to a stop behind us, and out stepped Himself.

"Boy, what the hell are you doing?"

"I am," I panted with great dignity, "trying to resolve a property dispute."

"I swear," he muttered, stepping around us. "Kids these days... WHOA!"

Long pause while the sheriff pinched the bridge of his nose and practiced breathing in through his nose and out through his mouth.

"Opal."

"Mister Randy?"

"Turn loose of Desmond."

"I done told Mister Dawg this ain't no concern of the law."

"I'm not going to argue with you, Opal. Drop that and get over here."

"Now, Mister Randy, that ain't fair," Opal's lip started trembling, and tears welled up in her eyes, "I feed him. I keep gas in his car. I give him a place to sleep at night. I want what's mine, and I'm keeping it. What he does is no concern of mine, but I'm keeping this."

The sheriff heaved the mighty sigh of a man who is unfairly beset by the evils of the world, wandered over to the bar ditch, and started kicking through the assorted stumps, branches, and planks while Opal glowered, Desmond wheezed, and I leaned against Opal's broad back and contemplated mutiny.

Apropos of nothing, the sheriff announced, "I hate tarantulas. Matter-of-fact, the only thing—ah-hah!—that I hate worse than a tarantula is one of those damned scorpions." On went his leather gloves, he swooped down and came back up with something cupped gingerly in his hands.

The sheriff wandered over to our little tableau.

"I mean, sure when you get bit by one of them big, hairy bastards, you fall down and froth at the mouth for a while, but for sheer screaming agony, a scorpion sting will do it every time."

"No," I thought, "Oh, hell, no."

"Opal," said the sheriff, gently, as he stopped next to me, "I'm not going to tell you again. You turn loose of Desmond, and you do it now."

"Now, Mister Randy–"

The sheriff reached out, hooked the collar of Opal's muumuu, and promptly dropped one of those big, blue, spiky, Texas cornfield locusts down the back of Opal's neck.

Folks, if I'm lying, I'm dying. Not only did Opal detach herself from Desmond's anatomy, she levitated six entire feet into the air, one arm going around the equator, and one taking the cross-polar route, hit the ground with a 4 on the Richter Scale, and took off down the street like a berserk cape buffalo, screaming for Big Mama every foot of the way.

The sheriff dusted off his hands and fixed me with a gimlet eye. "Now what did I tell you about working smarter, not harder?"

FILE 6
Box o' Steaks

I had watched some police procedural in which the main character was chasing yet another criminal mastermind and then publicly lamented that appalling lack of an Evil Genius in my career. Pretty soon the discussion devolved into a "Just How Stupid Are They, Really?" affair, and this story was born.

Other than the blurring of details and some minor Poetic License to camouflage the identities of all involved, this story is—my paw to God—accurate. Most officers that I've talked to have a story about a criminal every bit as stupid as this one. Heck, I've met a couple of officers who have read this story and swear—not realizing that I am the author—that they were the Bubba mentioned below.

They weren't, but the fact that they think they were just goes to reinforce the idea that this particular episode of "Derp" is not unique.

Oh, and the initial two sentences you see here were added a couple of hours after I posted it on my blog in an attempt to head off the inevitable charges of racism. It didn't work.

There's nothing quite like getting ambushed by a buzzard to let you know that your week is about to take a header down the khazi.

Especially when the buzzard is the size of a Boeing jet and made out of ballpoint pen ink.

I had walked into the main room of The Feedlot in search of nothing more exciting than a chicken-fried steak dinner and a gallon of iced tea, but the main room of the restaurant seemed to have been replaced by a jailhouse tattoo of a buzzard staring down into a bloody huge canyon of cleavage.

I took a couple of steps back, looked up, and groped for my pepper spray as Pearl, Big Mama's youngest daughter and Opal's baby sister, squinted down at me through the haze of smoke generated by the panetela cigar dangling from the side of her mouth.

"Mister 'Dog," said Pearl, removing the stogie and thumping about two inches of ash onto the carpet, "Put'cher butt inna seat. You drinkin'?"

"Pearl!" I heard the voice of the restaurant's owner.

Pearl sighed, rolled her eyes at the ceiling, replaced her panetela, and while making suggestive pumping gestures with a closed fist, fingers tattooed with the word "l U V F", she sing-songed, "Welcome-to-the-Feedlot-smoking-over-there-non-smoking-over-there-would-you-like-something-to-drink?"

I stood there for a moment, taking in the miniskirt, fishnet stockings, engineer boots, and spaghetti-strap halter top that revealed enough pen ink to be a monument to the Bic Corporation, not to mention waaa-aay too much of six-foot, four-inch, 340-plus pounds of Pearl.

"What?" she grunted, planting a fist, this one bearing the word "H a 7 F", on one hip.

"Umm," sayeth I, more than a bit flabbergasted, "You got a job?"

"Yeah," she snarled, "Mother[deleted] down at the parole office got a little [deleted] an' tryin' to prove he a man. Told me I hadda get a job, or he gonna revoke my [deleted]."

"The horror."

"Got that [deleted] right." She turned and clomped off through the tables.

I made my way to my usual seat and was subsequently joined by Joe Bob, the owner of The Feedlot.

"You've got to do something."

"I am going to do something. I'm going to eat a chicken-fried steak."

"No, Dog, you've got to do something about her," he jerked a surreptitious thumb at Pearl, who was fishing around for something elbow-deep in her bra, "She's driving off my business."

Pearl jerked a Kleenex from the depths of her decolletage, gave it a brief examination, and dropped it onto a table next to a formerly napkin-less customer.

"Private contracts between private citizens are not my business, Joe Bob. You hired her. You want her fired. You do it."

"Now, see here, Dog, my taxes pay your salary..."

"Yes," I interrupted, "Your taxes pay about 1/5500th of my salary. That's about five dollars per year. Here's your five bucks worth: in a fight, Pearl goes for the wedding tackle. You might want to keep that in mind."

We watched in silence as Pearl picked up a plate in front of a customer, cocked a finger under her thumb, flicked something off the plate, and thumped the plate back down in front of the customer.

"Do you want me to beg?"

"I'm not going to fire your employee. That's your job."

"I'm begging you."

"Nope."

"I'll pay you."

"Not going to happen."

There was a long silence that was finally broken when the other waitress set my steak dinner in front of me.

"If she kills me, where are you going to go for another steak like that, huh?"

I chewed appreciatively, "To whichever diner hires your cook."

"You'll be sorry when I'm dead."

"I'll cry and tell nice lies about you at the funeral. Pass the pepper, please."

Joe Bob snarled wordlessly at me and stomped off to his office.

To my surprise, dinner was uneventful, especially compared to my previous run-ins with Pearl. The rest of the shift was quiet, and I went to bed happy.

About 0445, the phone rang.

"Mmhprg, drizl?"

"'Dog," said the midnight dispatcher, "We've had a break-in at The Feedlot. Sheriff said to meet him there."

"Unkfd."

I threw on some clothes and pulled up in front of The Feedlot about the same time as the sheriff. Bubba, the night deputy, and Joe Bob met us at the door.

"I checked the alley at 0300, and the door was shut," said Bubba, altogether too cheerful for that early in the morning, "I came back at 0430, and the door was standing open. I've cleared the inside, and Joe Bob says the only thing missing is three boxes of steaks from the walk-in freezer."

I squinted at Joe Bob, "Did you fire her?"

"Who?" grunted the sheriff.

"Yeah," grouched Joe Bob, "I fired her last night at closing. No thanks to you, by the way."

"He hired Big Mama's Pearl as a waitress," I said to my boss. "Decided he made a mistake and wanted me to fire her for him."

"Moron," grunted Himself, although it was unclear to whom he was referring. "Anybody know where Pearl is staying these days? I think we might want to have a chat with that girl."

As if on cue, a 1970-something Primer Gray Buick Doorless pulled into the parking lot of The Feedlot, and Pearl eased out of the driver's seat through the gaping hole where the door used to be.

"'Mornin', Mr. Randy, Mr. Joe Bob. I done heard about the thievin', and I know some people who know some people, and I thought since you was a nice man 'n' all, I'd get you a couple'a box of steaks to replace the ones that done got stoled" said Pearl, just as chipper as all hell.

She lifted two white boxes out of the back of the Buick and placed them on the trunk lid.

"Now, Pearl," murmured the sheriff, laying a hand on a box, "That's almighty neighborly of you."

I'm sure that it was random chance that caused the sheriff's hand to cover the orange-and-white sticker that read: "Deliver to The Feedlot, Bugscuffle, Texas."

I nodded, wandering up on the other side of Pearl.

"Hey," said Joe Bob, "That's... OW!"

"Sorry, sheriff," said Bubba, "I seem to have accidentally stepped upon Joe Bob's foot."

"Now, Mr. Joe Bob, I done bought these here boxes at twenny dolla's each. Just to show there ain't no hard feelin's 'tween you 'n' me and 'cause you is in a bad way right now, I'll sell 'em to you at twenny each. I won't take no profit 'cause I like you."

"Well, now, Pearl," smiled the sheriff, "That doesn't seem hardly right. Tell you what we're going to do. Seeing as how Mr. Joe Bob can't lock up his place, we'll take these steaks down to the office, so they'll be safe. While we're there, I'm going to write you a receipt for the boxes, and we'll get the town Good Samaritan Fund to pay you fifty dollars for this good deed."

"That's awful nice of you, Mr. Randy," Pearl said as Bubba gathered up the boxes and put them in the back seat of his cruiser.

I smiled real big at Pearl and held open the back door of the sheriff's cruiser, as with every indication of courtesy and manners, the sheriff gently took her arm, patted her hand, and led her to his car.

We were just about in the clear when Joe Bob ruined everything.

"Are you blind?" bellowed Joe Bob, as he waved one of the stickers from the steak boxes in our general direction, "These are my own [deleted] steaks! Are you [deleted] stupid enough to pay her for the [deleted] steaks she [deleted] STOLE?!"

sigh

Things went rodeo from there.

Pearl planted her feet as the sheriff attempted to shove her inside the backdoor of the cruiser, I jumped forward and snagged a good grip on her other arm, and Bubba came sprinting at us, unlimbering his can of OC.

I fired a solid knee-strike into Pearl's thigh with the intention of distracting her, but she was apparently too busy smacking the sheriff across the parking lot to notice. Seeing as how Plan A was well-and-truly paws-up, I kneed Pearl a second time and attempted a takedown.

Unfortunately, right after I threw the knee, I felt her arm straighten out, and then she got my full and complete attention, along with a huge pawful of the bifurcation of my jeans.

She yanked up, and I was more than happy to jump whichever way she was wanting to go. Unfortunately, I bobbled the landing a bit and hit the parking lot at Pearl's feet.

Bubba lined up on Pearl's face with his can of OC, but held fire as the sheriff jumped up onto Pearl's back and snaked an arm around her neck. She dug her chin into her chest, blocking the sheriff's choke, reached out for a pawful of Bubba's face, and proceeded to throw him bodily across the parking lot. Then, she turned and started lumbering toward her car.

Seeing no other choice, I reached up and wrapped both my arms around her leg, forcing her to drag me along. She took about four steps and then stopped to try to pull the sheriff off her back, so I took the opportunity to weasel my slapper out of my vest pocket. She started dragging me in a circle, trying to shake me off while I held on for dear life.

Bubba pulled himself out of the gravel, took a couple of steps, and then kicked the hell out of Pearl's other leg, rocking her and giving me the chance to wrap my legs around her leg and to start beating the absolute whey out of her thigh with my slapper.

Between Bubba kicking at her left leg, me wrapped like a rabid spider monkey around her right leg and pounding on it with a lead weight, and the sheriff furiously trying to lock in that choke hold, it was only about another five minutes before Pearl finally gave up the fight.

We got her 'cuffed and stuffed into the back of the sheriff's cruiser, and were taking stock of our various injuries, when Joe Bob bounced over, just as excited as a litter of puppies.

"Holy [deleted]! That was better'n Monday Night Wrasslin'! That was like a comic book! Wow!"

"Joe Bob," muttered the sheriff, trying to staunch a nose that was gushing with blood. "You are a moron. I oughta flat whip your butt. Go home, get something to lock your diner up with, and come get your steaks at the office later. Let's go."

Believe it or not, that was the shortest serious fight we ever had with one of Big Mama's offspring.

FILE 7
Two Beers

If you ask anyone who's been in Law Enforcement long enough to wear the first coat of polish off of his boots, he'll tell you about "Two Beers."

It's pretty much a trope.

Somebody needs to show me these two beers.

I have heard about them all of my law enforcement career, usually at about 3 o'clock in the morning, but it's obvious that someone is actively engaged in hiding them from me.

There I was, driving along minding my own business, when I noticed the bed of a pickup truck sticking out of a house.

Now, this is the sort of thing that naturally draws an observant cop's attention, what with our training and all, so I stopped and got out to ponder the architectural statement of a bloody huge Ford tailgate protruding from between a couple of very large bay windows.

As I meditated upon this, I notice a pair of trenches cut into the lawn that led from the street to the pickup truck.

This discovery, together with the bisected hedge and the mysterious disappearance of the Mama Deer lawn ornament that had previously been located between the Daddy Deer to the left of the trenches and Baby Bambi on the right, caused me to believe that my professional services were probably required.

I called dispatch and had them run a 10-28 on the license plate prominently attached to the visible part of the pickup, then further informed them that I required the services of the Volunteer Fire Department, a mentally flexible tow-truck driver, and possibly EMS.

After that, I scrambled up onto the bed of the pickup, ducked under the collapsed eaves, and crab-crawled into the living room.

The first thing I noticed in the glare of the one remaining headlight was Mama Deer looking at me reproachfully from somewhere betwixt the radiator and the fuel pump.

The second thing was the gentleman who was steadying himself against a bookcase with one hand, warbling a country song as he relieved himself into some kind of potted plant.

Ah, I think to myself, here is Person of Interest Number One! It's all that training, you see.

I looked into the cab of the pickup, but I didn't see anyone else. Behind me, George Strait left his saddle in San Antone, and I padded into the kitchen.

A quick twist of the taps produced no water. I remembered that the owners of this house were summering in Colorado, and it looked like they hadn't come back yet.

A quick trip through the bedrooms revealed only dust and a musty smell, thank God, so I returned to Mama Deer and Person of Interest Number One, just as dispatch returned the name and address of the registered owner of the pickup.

I approached the gentleman, who was occupied with firmly levering an unoffending branch up and down, from behind and I cleared my throat.

"What's on your mind, sir?"

"Summbeesch won-wonn—won't flusdht."

"That's okay, sir, ferns are bad that way. Want to tell me what happened here?"

"Welsh, I's tak-taken a whizz, 'n the thin-thingie won't fllushdt."

"Ah," I say, "And how much have you had to drink tonight?'

Behind my back, I extended two fingers.

He looked at his own hand, counted unsteadily, and then waved a victory sign at me.

"T-two beersh!"

Damn, I'm good. I should give lessons to Miss Cleo.

"You do realize, sir, that you have succeeded in parking your truck in a house?"

"G'wan funnymaansh... wa-wait minnit. Yoosh a copdt."

Hello, higher brain functions! I waved the flashlight beam around the living room, revealing the pickup grill, the various bits and pieces dangling from the ceiling. The decapitated plaster deer.

"Oh-o-oh, chidt."

"Succinct, yet pithy observation. Let's go outside."

"Way, way, wayminnit! Yoush 'rrestin' me? Whafor?"

"Suspected DWI and hunting plaster deer out of season."

"Nonono, no. Mansh got ri', rite to do wha he wnats wi' his hoo-hou-housh!"

"Yes!" I exclaim, happily, "Yes, he does! And you are Mr. Jim Drunkard, of Onehorse, Texas, are you not?!"

"Yeesh! Da's me!"

"This is Bugscuffle. Onehorse is about 120 miles that way." Being a helpful public servant, I indicated the direction.

"Oh. Chidt."

I want to see the two beers that can give a 270-pound man a BAC of 0.27 percent.

Seriously. Do they come in buckets or what? Is there a secret non-cop beer mug measured in gallons stashed behind every bar?

FILE 8
The Six-Foot Chickens

Benny is the subject of several of my stories, along with his perpetually pregnant wife, Jolene. Both of them were as meek as church mice right up until Benny got into the tequila. Which he did about once a month. Once he was good and liquored up, Benny would get depressed and attempt to off himself, but the traditional ways were never good enough for Benny. He'd lay down in front of a farmer's hay bailer, chain himself to train tracks which hadn't seen a train in a hundred years, or try to drown himself in two inches of water.

Which would lead to one of us—usually me—arresting the five-foot-nothing Benny for "Fooblic Intoxidation." This was reliably followed by Jolene attempting to defend her husband and going berserk.

Considering that Jolene was, as noted, usually pregnant and about four feet, eight inches tall, we usually attempted to avoid putting Jolene in jail. Not always successfully, however.

———

There I was, parked in the Allsup's lot with an an extra-jumbo Dr. Pepper in one paw and a chimichanga in the other. Somewhere else in the county, a rookie officer was doing his first solo patrol. Life was good.

"SO, car 12."

Chomp, chomp "Go ahead."

"Car 12, car 20 requests backup at Wobble Creek. He's nekkid."

I paused, for a moment, eyeing my chimichanga suspiciously, and then keyed the mic: "Car 12, SO. Say again your last?" *Please, please let me be hallucinating.*

"Car 12, I'm just relaying what I was told. The kid needs help and said he was nekkid."

I hightailed it to the location, looked frantically for the rookie's cruiser, and spotted it parked beside a big corral. I whipped in beside the corral, leaped out, and started looking for my newbie. All I saw was a rancher leaning against the corral, chewing on a stalk of something, and staring with bemused fascination into the corral. I looked into the corral, and it was full of chickens. *Six-foot-tall* chickens.

"T'ain't chickens," grunted the rancher before I could say anything. "Emus."

I was about to ask what an Australian bird was doing in North Texas, and then I noticed that about four of these mutant chickens were in one corner of the pen, crawling all over each other and trying to get away from a man in the center of the pen.

A man who was on his knees, arms held out in supplication to the terrified megafowl, and begging in alcohol-sodden tones, "Birdie want a Benny?"

And he was as utterly, completely, and totally bare-butt nekkid as the day he was born.

On the other side of the corral was my rookie. He was crawling frantically for the corral fence while an enraged six-foot chicken jumped up and down on his back.

It was a Prozac moment.

"Frank." Could those calm tones belong to me? "Would you mind getting out here? Thank you. Benny, come here. Now."

Benny turned and shuffled toward me with an air of I've-done-something-wrong-but-I-don't-know-what-it-is-yet while staying well out of grabbing range.

Still wondering where this remarkable calm came from, I asked, "Benny, what are you doing in that chicken coop?"

"T'aint chickens. Emus" grunted the rancher.

Benny warbled, hiccuped, and waved his arms at me.

"You're doing what? Committing *suicide*? *BY CHICKEN?*"

Frank had managed to reach the top bar of the corral, but right about then he was jerked loose and suplexed back into the corral by the emu, which appeared to have World Wrestling Federation aspirations.

That nice, calm feeling totally evaporated.

"Frank! Quit screwing around with that chicken and get out here! Benny. Get. Over. Here. Now!"

"T'aint a chicken. Emu."

Benny, still on his knees, shuffled toward me an inch at a time, his lower lip quivering pitifully. As soon as he was close enough, I got an arm around him... and slipped right off him. I stared at my suddenly greasy arm, looked closer at Benny, and saw that he was covered in bacon grease.

Apparently, he wanted to taste good when they pecked him to death.

Bloody considerate of him. Too bad six-foot chickens don't like bacon. The rancher stared at Benny for a moment and then collapsed against the fence, pounding it with his fist and howling with laughter.

Frank crawled out from under the lowest bar of the fence just in time to catch an airborne Benny as I forcibly removed his naked, bacon-greased body from the corral.

FILE 9

Fooblic Intoxidation

Benny, again.

A few years back I was passing through my old stomping grounds, stopped in Bugscuffle for a burger, and came across some local residents. I had figured that after a couple of decades, no one there would remember me, but apparently I made more of an impression than I had thought.

During the course of the conversation, I learned that Benny had Passed On. I thought that one of his hare-brained drunken suicide schemes had finally paid off, but no, he was at work, sober, when a massive myocardial infarction got him. Thankfully, he never knew what hit him.

I wouldn't have thought that the death of a drunk I had arrested multiple times twenty years ago would have hit me quite so hard, but I found I was genuinely upset when I heard of his passing.

Odd, that.

Late one evening—or early one morning, depending on your frame of reference—Dispatch got a prowler call from one of our lake residents.

I scooted out there, started looking around, and discovered something kind of weird. There was an 18-inch-wide strip of ground going up the driveway that looked like it had been roto-tilled, but it was only about an inch deep.

A bit puzzled, I followed the strip of torn-up earth up the drive-way, onto the front lawn, through the hedge, down the side lot, up a gentle hill, down the backside of the hill, across a miniature beach, and up onto a dilapidated boat dock.

At the far end of the dock, a small figure was bent over, hands on knees, apparently trying to choose between wheezing and hic-cuping beside a fairly substantial pile of something unidentifi-able.

sigh

Being careful to avoid the torn-up planks, I stepped onto the dock and meandered down to the figure at the far end.

"Evening, Benny" I said, as I extracted a stick of gum from my vest, "What's on your mind?"

Benny waved, gurgled, and hiccuped solemnly at me. I took the opportunity to examine the mysterious pile, which turned out to be about six cinder blocks which had been chained together and locked with a rusty padlock. Half-inch rope had been carefully, and thoroughly, knotted to the chain, with about twenty feet of its length neatly coiled on the dock before being knotted, again carefully and *most* thoroughly, around Benny's right ankle.

It was a Migraine Salute Moment.

"Benny," I said, gently, as a headache thundered up my spine and flowered beautifully behind my eyes, "What the Hell are you doing this time?"

Benny blinked and then explained his plan to cast himself into the briny deep so that he would no longer be an embarrassment to his wife and family.

I shined my flashlight over the edge of the dock. Cracked black mud baked sullenly in the heat of a Texas evening. I swung the light up to Benny and then back down. Still mud. My gum made a faint, but convincing thud as it landed on the ground, one hundred feet from anything resembling water.

This was one for the notebooks.

"Benny," I began, drawing in a breath for what I intended to be a truly epic dressing-down, "This is absolutely the—"

I paused because Benny had drawn up both fists pugnaciously and was waving them in front of his face as he swayed gently back and forth on the dock.

Bloody Hell.

"All right, Benny," I sighed. "You want some help?"

Benny paused for a moment as the thought burbled its way through the tequila-sodden depths of his conscious before striking home and causing Benny to nod vigorously.

"Okay. Lift! On three! One, two, three! Three, Benny! Three!"

I waved away the small puff of dust raised by the impact of the cinder blocks and then turned to see Benny offering me a small paw. We shook hands, and then Benny patted me gently on the arm, took two deep breaths, held the third, pinched his nose shut, and screwed his eyes closed.

And waited.

I opened another stick of gum. Sighed. Pulled out my pocket-knife and cut the rope. Put away the pocketknife. Stood beside the gently swaying Benny. Contemplated the life of a small-town deputy.

After a minute or so, Benny's eyes opened, and he looked at me in utter confusion, wondering I guess, where the water was.

I waggled my fingers at him. Benny closed his eyes again. I gave him about another minute before I whacked him firmly between the shoulder blades, barking, "Breathe, Benny!"

Benny almost collapsed as he drew a massive breath. I lowered my shoulder, which let him fall into a nice little fireman's carry and started walking toward my cruiser.

"I swear to God, Benny!"

"Fooblic... *wheeze* ... Intoxidation?"

"Damned skippy Fooblic Intoxidation. Again."

FILE 10

Pheasant Season

Getting sprinkled with bird shot during hunting season isn't as rare as one might think. However, the closer-in incidents are very rare.

Insert appropriate Dick Cheney joke here. I'd like to go on the record as having written this several years before the VPOTUS decided to bag his limit on lawyers.

The really absurd part of this story is that the same two players in this one did almost the exact same thing about eight months later. Only, the second time, they pulled up to the sheriff's office while a van-load of federal types were doing their once-a-year show-the-flag tour to the outlying counties. Fun times.

By the by, translating English into Injured Redneck is more difficult than one might think.

Ahem.

I had been out west of town settling a dispute concerning the paternity of a litter of puppies and was heading back to the SO on one of those lovely Panhandle fall afternoons. I had the window down and was just generally enjoying myself when I was passed by a 1958 Chevy pickup doing approximately twice the legal speed limit.

sigh

About ten miles later, I got the Chevy pulled over, when the driver got out and sprinted back to the cruiser. Friends of mine can tell you that I have a real dislike for people doing that, so I promptly tore into him:

"Nug, what the hell are you doing?"

"Well," he said, scrunching and fidgeting with his gimme hat, "I done murdered Dobie, and I thought I might oughta find a doctor for him."

"Do you realize how fast you were going? All four of these tires are so bald that they're showing wire, the passenger side front fender is going to fly off in the wind... Wait. You did what?"

Nug's expression kind of wrinkled up, and he mauled his cap a bit more. "I kilt Dobie."

Oh, God. This, I didn't need. I found myself speaking very slowly and carefully, "Nug, are you sure you killed Dobie?"

"We-eeell, I shot him in the face with a shotgun."

Oh, yeah. That'll do the trick. I felt a headache tip-toeing its way up my spine with all the dainty grace of a rhino in steel-toed combat boots.

"Nug," said I, still in that slow, calm voice, "Think carefully now. Did you mean to shoot your brother?"

He abruptly took on a hunted expression. His hands clutched convulsively at the John Deere cap; he knew there was a legal trick somewhere in my words. He sought a neutral, non-condemning answer, an answer which wouldn't violate his Fifth Amendment Rights. He had it!

"You mean, this time?"

sigh

"One felony at a time, Nug. And where's the body?"

Nug looked at the truck, "He's in the back."

I pointed at Nug, "Don't go anywhere!" Then, I vaulted onto the rear bumper of the truck, and sure enough, we had a body lying on a bed of fish poles, beer cans, oil jugs, shotgun shells, and other assorted detritus necessary for the proper operation of a country truck. And, even better, the corpus had slid forward far enough that everything from the armpits up was hidden under the toolbox.

Oh, joy. I swallowed a couple of times, took a deep breath, latched onto the ankles of the cadaver, and began to pull him out from under the toolbox, when the Deceased promptly spasmed violently in my grip, such spasm together with the deep, sonorous tone of a bell sounding in a place where there weren't any bells, which caused me to turn loose the ankles of the Dearly Departed and to tumble into the bar ditch.

Okay. No problem.

I was laying there in the bar-ditch, pulling goat-head stickers out of my limbs and very carefully not wondering about how much a face being slammed into the bottom of a stainless-steel toolbox sounded remarkably like a church bell, when said face appeared over the edge of the pickup bed and peered down at me in an accusatory fashion.

"Ju brogd by dode."

I concentrated on removing a particularly ambitious sticker.

"By ond brugga choosts be in de ged, and deen de gops breg by dode."

I rolled to my feet carefully ambled back to the cruiser, and fished around in the back seat until I found a handkerchief, walked back to the pickup, and handed it to Dobie.

"Thakds" he mumbled, dabbling the blood flowing down his face and revealing several dozen dark gray pimples. They were suspiciously leaden in color.

I sat on the bumper, fishing around in my vest for a badly needed stick of gum, "Hunting accident?" I hazarded, minutely studying a paleolithic stick of Juicy Fruit clutched in my ever-so-slightly trembling paw.

"Dumg fezant tookt off betweeg us, and by dumg chit brugga wagn't looging where he was chooging."

"Quail, Dobie," I said very firmly. "Pheasant season is still a couple of weeks away."

"Dugn't magger. By dumg chit brugga goodn't git a bull in de bugt widt a figgle angyway."

I look at Nug, who was cogitating intently, "That about what happened, Nug?"

"I'm pretty sure it was a pheasant," opined Nug reflectively. "It had a long tail and a ring around its neck, and it was a lot bigger than one of them little quail."

"Nug, don't say anything. Now, nod your head. No, keep nodding. Did you accidentally shoot your brother while hunting birds? Good. Take Dobie to the doctor and get him patched up."

"Dumg chit brugga goona neeg a goctor agger I gicg his bugt."

"Oh, yeah? You and which army?"

Which was the last thing I heard as I abandoned the two intrepid huntsmen and went in search of a badly needed, soothing cup of tea.

FILE 11

Communion

This story isn't funny, but it is one of my favorites. Being a Peace Officer, particularly one in a small town, isn't anything like what you see on the TeeVee.

Well, it's a bit like Barney Miller. A little bit.

It's actually a lot more like this story: a little bittersweet, with no real rewards besides that warm little feeling at the end of the day.

"Really," I said, trying to fit as much disbelief and sarcasm as possible into those two syllables.

"Yes, sir."

I stared at the 16-year-old boy for a good while before allowing my eyebrow to lift.

"You're visiting your girlfriend, whose last name you can't quite recall at this time, whose first name is either Stacey or Shelly depending on when you're asked, and you're not sure what her address is, but it is—and let me quote this—"On a street'."

Long pause.

"Umm… yeah?"

"Ah. And as far as romantic gifts go, your lady is perfectly happy with a gym bag packed with," I pulled each object out one at a time, "a ski mask, a pair of leather work gloves, and—goodness— a crowbar!"

The kid was looking at everything in the vicinity except me.

"We all need to be honest here, so let me be the first: You, sir, are a thief. Ah! Let me finish. The fact that you do not have a criminal history attached to your name merely tells me that you are a heretofore lucky thief. You're not here to visit your girlfriend because any girl young enough to be dating you will be at tonight's homecoming football game. Where, coincidentally enough, much of the rest of the town is located. Which leads us to yourself, wandering the empty streets all by your lonesome with naught but a bag of burglar's tools to keep you company."

I could hear him swallow, so I took a step forward, crowding his personal space.

"So there are two ways this is going to settle out. The first is that I take you and your stuff back to the office, I call the football stadium, and when a member of the West Podunk High School faculty shows up, I tell him what I think is going on, give him you and your bag of goodies, and wave bye-bye."

I didn't think he liked that idea.

"The second way is that I hand you this receipt for your bag of burglar's tools, you take yourself back to the stadium, and I don't see hide or hair of you outside that stadium for the rest of the evening. Tomorrow, you bring that receipt and a parent to the office, and I give you back your crowbar, your gloves, and your ski-mask."

I guessed from the nodding that the second choice was a bit more palatable.

"Five blocks that way. You can't miss the lights. Scram."

sigh

Hopefully, he had gotten enough of a scare to persuade him that the critter life wasn't for him. Yeah, and as long as I was hoping, could I get a long-legged lingerie model with a bag of grapes? I filed the fink card—excuse me "Field Interview Card"—in the Bloody Idiots file in my briefcase and cleared the call.

It was one of those lovely fall Panhandle evenings, so about ten minutes later I parked the Super Scooter at the end of Second Street, got out, and started checking doors on what passed as the Main Business District of Bugscuffle, Texas.

Three doors later, I smiled slightly as a roar echoed lightly around the front porch. A moment later, the sounds of musical instruments played maybe with a little more enthusiasm than skill followed. Sounded like the Bugscuffle Fighting Rednecks were doing well this evening.

I pushed gently on the door I was facing… and it swung open. Crap.

"Car 12, County."

"Go ahead, 12."

"I've an open door at 1201 Second Street. Public service the Williams and see if they can put an eyeball on Dot."

There's more than a touch of amusement in dispatch's voice as she replies, "10-4, 12. You want me to roll you some backup?"

Minx.

"Negative, County," I said as I stepped into the front hall of the Conroe and Conroe Funeral Home, "I'll be on the portable."

A dollar will get you a doughnut that I was going to find the same thing I'd found the last umpteen Open Door calls we'd gotten here, but I was well aware that Murphy hated my guts—personally. So my P7 was hidden behind my leg, finger indexed along the frame as I shined my Surefire through the business office, the guest rooms, multiple viewing rooms, the Icky Room, casket storage, finally to be slipped back into the holster as I found the small, slim figure sitting all alone in the chapel.

Dot Williams was dressed in her standard uniform of hot pink sneakers, blue jeans, and Hello Kitty sweatshirt, one foot swinging idly as she gravely regarded the awful plastic gold-painted, flower-adorned abstract sculpture stuck to the wall behind the altar. In honor of the evening's football game, a red-and-black football was painted on one cheek, and red and silver ribbons had been threaded into her ever-present ponytail.

Eleven years ago, a college kid with a one-ton Western Hauler pickup truck and a blood alcohol concentration of 0.22 packed the Chevy S-10 driven by the hugely pregnant Mrs. Williams into a little bitty mangled ball and bounced it across Main Street. The Bugscuffle Volunteer Fire Department earned their Christmas hams that evening in as deft a display of the Fine Art of Power Extrication as any department, paid or volunteer, could hope for. A couple of hours after the Jaws of Life were cleaned and stored, Dorothy Elise Williams was born.

I scraped my boot heels on the carpet as I walked around the end of the pew, being careful not to startle the little girl, although, truth be known, I had no idea if Dot had ever been startled in her life. Or if it was even possible to startle her. Then I sat quietly on the bench just within arms' reach and pondered the sculpture.

Yeah. It was bloody awful.

I reached into my vest and pulled out a pack of chewing gum, unwrapped a stick and chewed for a bit before taking a second stick out of the pack and—careful not to look at Dot—casually laid it on the bench midway between us. A couple of breaths later, equally casually, and without taking her eyes off the plastic abomination on the wall, Dot reached out and took the stick, unwrapping it with ferocious concentration and putting it into her mouth one quarter piece at a time before meticulously folding the foil wrapper into little squares and laying it on the bench midway between us. After a couple of breaths, I carefully picked it up and stuck it in an inner pocket of my denim vest.

Dot is odd.

Probably not very long after I sat down, but considerably longer than I would have liked—I was sitting in a funeral home, after dark, and I had seen this movie—Dot slid a battered something or other that I think was probably once a stuffed giraffe along the pew toward me, while maintaining a firm grip on one of its appendages with her left hand.

Careful not to touch the little girl, I grabbed a hold of a fuzzy limb and then carefully stood up. A beat later, Dot stood up herself, and then we started walking toward the exit.

Dot doesn't like to be touched. As a matter of fact, the only sound I've ever heard the wee sprite make is an ear-splitting shriek whenever someone who isn't family touches her. Learning that lesson left my ears ringing for days. However, as various and sundry gods are my witnesses, I swore that if this little girl turned and waved at the altar, I was picking her up and carrying her out the door at a dead sprint, probably emptying my magazine over my shoulder as we go, banshee wails and damage complaints notwithstanding.

Like I said, I've seen that movie.

Fortunately, anything Dot might have been communing with seemed to lack an appreciation for social graces or simply wished to spare my overactive imagination, and there was no waving.

When we stepped out onto the front porch, an elderly man who had been leaning against the guard rail cleared his throat. Not really necessary, but polite all the same.

"Bert," I said to the owner of Conroe and Conroe Funeral Home. "Thought you'd be at the game instead of listening to the scanner."

He grinned. "I was. Sitting next to the sheriff on the fifty-yard line when I heard the call over his radio."

Ah.

"I doubt that anything is missing or damaged—" He raised a hand, cutting me off.

"Of course not. Dot would never be that crass." He gave a formal Southern nod off to my left, and I realized that I was the only one holding onto the stuffed wossname. Bloody Hell.

"Miss Dot. How are you this evening?"

Dot, who was intently examining a mimosa branch at the end of the porch, ignored him. He smiled and then moved to shut and lock the door.

"Dorothy Elise Williams!" On the street, a Suburban had pulled to a stop, catty-wampus, before disgorging Mr. and Mrs. Williams, the latter of whom was heading for her youngest at full speed. "What have I told you about wandering off, young lady!"

"'Bert, 'Dog, I'm so sorry!" Cody Williams had taken off his Stetson and was wringing the brim. I'm a little shocked. "We were talking to the new pastor and just took our eyes off of her for a second!"

I wave the stuffed whatsit at him, "Cody. Put your hat back on. You look weird without it. No blood, no foul."

Albert Conroe smiled at him genially. "We've had this talk before, Cody. It's quiet, she likes it, and she's a very courteous guest. I don't have an issue."

At the end of the porch, Mrs. Williams had taken her daughter's chin and gently turned her to make eye contact. There was an amount of finger-shaking going on when Dot reached out and very gently patted her mother on the cheek before turning her attention back to the branch.

I handed Cody the stuffed thingie. "Take your family back to the game."

Bert and I stood on the porch as the Williams climbed into the Suburban and took off.

Bert chuckled gently, "Small towns."

Yep.

FILE 12

Going Home

This is the second-most-popular story I've ever written.

After a bad day at work, I had intended to sit down and write something amusing to de-stress, but this came out. Usually when I write, there is a great deal of cutting-and-pasting, I'll read and reread several times, changing entire sections on a whim, but that wasn't the case with this one.

I wrote the entire thing in a single rush, just as you see it now, and was quite frankly exhausted when I was done. I read it once and thought it was a decent retelling of the actual event but felt that it didn't quite make the cut for posting.

I have written several stories—darker in tone, or violent, or sad— that I don't think fit the overall tone of my site, so I put them into the Drafts folder.

It seems I was tired enough that I hit "Publish" when I meant "Save" before pushing my chair back and collapsing into bed. When I checked my site the next day, the statistics had gone wild.

I have been accused of embellishing this story a bit as some think it's too Hollywood. Sorry, but other than blurring the identifying details, this is probably the least tampered-with story I've written. Not even the editor of this book has touched it.

"Car 10" is the radio call-sign of the Sheriff. I was "Car 12."

"County, car 12."

"12, go ahead."

"12, when you go 10-8, contact the supervisor at 2300 Fernoak Road."

I stared at the cows I was currently attempting to put back behind their fence. Crap. Crap crap crap.

Twenty minutes later I pulled up to the back door of the local nursing home.

I say back door, but it was actually a set of French doors on the back side of the dining room/TeeVee room, opening onto a patio, surrounded by a faux wrought-iron fence about eight feet high.

Just inside the fence, a matronly-looking woman in scrubs, body language giving every impression of annoyed impatience I had ever seen, looked pointedly at her wristwatch as I parked the cruiser.

"It's five minutes past seven o'clock. I called the sheriff at a quarter 'til. Be sure you put that in your report."

"Sorry about that, but I was on the far side of the county with a herd of cows when the—"

"That's sheriff's business. Mr. Johnson is missing. He's ninety-four years old, white, last seen wearing a tartan dressing robe over blue pajamas."

"Okay, good to know. When was he last seen?" Ninety-plus years old, I doubted that he had gotten further than, say, a mile. Unless someone had picked him up...

"What?"

"When was he last seen?"

"Are you implying something?"

What the hell? I looked at her over my Gargoyles in absolute confusion, "When was the last time he was seen? So I'll have a search limit?"

"Young man, Bugscuffle is not that big."

I saw how this one was going to be played. "Okay, do you have any idea which way he might have gone or where he might be going?"

"Mr. Johnson has a severe case of Alzheimer's. Not only do we not know where he may be going, or which way, but he doesn't know either." The 'you idiot' was unspoken.

I was trying not to show teeth in a smile that neither one of us was going to believe was friendly. "I understand. Can you tell me what kind of footwear he's wearing?"

"You, young man, should be looking for Mr. Johnson, not standing here, conducting what my lawyer will probably tell me is an illegal interro—"

"Madam. These are dirt streets. We haven't had rain in months, and there's a good layer of dust everywhere. I can track Mr. Johnson quite easily if I know what I'm looking for. Now. Am I looking for slippers, am I looking for sneakers, am I looking for bare feet, what?"

She looked at me for a long moment, no doubt cataloging my series of sins and trespasses in her mind.

"I'm sure that an aide will be able to help you. I'll send one out. You are planning on looking for poor Mr. Johnson sometime today, I hope?"

The amount of saccharine in that one little sentence would probably kill half a lab quota of rats, and I felt my jaw muscles knot up as I gravely inclined my head, "I'll certainly do my best. May I see Mr. Johnson's room?"

"He's not—oh, bother. Very well. 105." With that, the supervisor threw up her arms and stomped back into the facility, me taking the moment to slip in the self-locking door behind her.

A couple of moments later I was at room 105.

I had been here before. About three weeks back, half-an-hour before the end of my shift, the ambulance was paged out to the nursing home. As was our policy, I had responded and had come to this room from the other direction to find it full of aides and nurses. The bed just inside the door had been empty, bed clothes thrown back as if the occupant had been taken out of the room. The far bed had had two of the staff attempting to resuscitate a tiny figure; then two of our local paramedics had button-hooked the door and taken over, only to gently shake their heads after a brief exam.

What was her name... Viola Faye Carter Johnson. I worked the escort for her funeral later that week. I closed my eyes, and I replayed my courtesy at the service in my mind:

Walked in through the side door. Waited at the door while my eyes adjusted and spoke with the funeral director about the route and location of the grave site. Walked through the line... grandchildren, grandchildren, daughter, son, son, ah-hah. Tall, barrel-chested, big-boned, but no muscle over the bones. Natty bowler hat on top of thin white hair, incredibly bright yellow-and-red feather tucked rakishly in the hat-band, white mustache, good gray suit, malacca cane leaning forgotten against the pew.

Complete and total dazed incomprehension in the blue eyes.

Got him. Now I knew who he was.

Out of habit I looked under the bed. Hey, it's happened before. No such luck this time, though.

I opened the closet door—no Mr. Johnson there—the clothes were hung with almost military precision, no gaps to show missing clothes. I was looking at a tiny framed pen and watercolor portrait of a woman on the bedside table when two younger women stepped through the door, one of them carrying a red, blue, and green checkered robe.

Well, he was not wearing a tartan bathrobe after all. I hoped he was still wearing the blue pajamas.

The portrait was a bit smudged and looked like it was bent or folded a time or two before being framed. It was a blonde woman, young, who was pulling a blue ribbon from her ponytail while looking levelly at the artist. It was well-done, drawn with love as well as skill. Dollar to a doughnut says Mr. Johnson was the artist. It has that feel.

The aides are clearly upset. Mr. Johnson seems to have been a favorite. He is a white male, tall—they're not sure how tall—and he's nice. And never a problem.

That's nice to know.

The only thing they think is missing from his room—aside from him—is his cane. The side door alarm beeped at the supper meal at five. They thought that was him, but truth be told, nobody was really sure when Mr. Johnson amscrayed.

Yeah, this one wasn't going to be easy.

I tipped my hat to the aides and started walking around outside the home, checking the dirt at each door. At the side door, I found it. It was not much—a circular imprint a little bigger than the diameter of a quarter in the dirt—but in my memory I see the tan rubber aftermarket tip someone had slid onto Mr. Johnson's cane. With the cane imprint as a marker, I could see the shiny spots where his cloth-soled slippers had pressed into the caliche, and it was fairly easy to track Mr. Johnson to Muir Road.

I marked the spot, hurried back to the Super Scooter, called in a BOLO (Be On the Look Out) for Mr. Johnson to dispatch, and then ran from the cruiser up to my mark and started slowly idling east on Muir Road, head hung out the window, watching the little rounds marks.

Six blocks later, I was starting to get worried. Muir Road goes straight east into Old Town, the original location of Bugscuffle. In the early 1900s, maybe teens, something had happened in Old Bugscuffle—fire, tornado, I'm not sure. Whatever it was, that entire section of town had picked up and moved west to its current location, leaving behind stone foundations and a few low, ruined walls, overgrown in eighty-some-odd years of salt cedar, pecan trees, ornamental trees run amuck, cane breaks, and other tree-type growth. Worst of all, Old Bugscuffle had red brick streets. Which New Bugscuffle happily—and mindlessly—runs a street sweeper down every other week.

Two blocks later, I watched helplessly as the little circles and the small shiny spots turned into red brick streets. Dammit, dammit, dammit... "Car 12, County."

"Go ahead, 12."

"County, I've lost track of that BOLO at Muir and Pecan. Might be a good idea to turn out the VFD."

"10-4, car 12."

"10, dispatch."

"Go ahead, 10."

"What's 12 got?"

I climbed out of the car as dispatch filled the sheriff in on our Missing Person, hoping that Mr. Johnson had veered from his course and had climbed up into the grass. No such luck. But I honestly didn't figure a 94-year-old man would get off on un-even grass when there was a perfectly nice brick road right there. Dammit. My walkie-talkie crackled to life.

"Car 10, car 12."

"Go ahead.

"You know that foundation slab about a block and a half east from your current location where the high school kids go to party?"

"10-4."

"That's the old Carter place. Next door to the east is the old Johnson place. Comprende?"

Bingo. I felt my chest ease a bit. "10-4, car 10, I'm en route."

"Good. Car 10, Dispatch, tone the Fire Department and have them meet me at the corner of Muir and Pecan."

Three quick breaths later, I pulled the cruiser to a stop on the red brick street. North of the road was a huge lot waist-deep in vegetation—where it wasn't shoulder deep or worse in salt cedars, rioting pyracantha—and a narrow path wending its way through the undergrowth. I scooted along the path, anxiously looking for—and not finding—those little rounds marks, but checking anyway. At the end of the patch—almost fifty yards back—was an enormous stone foundation slab.

Dozens of burn marks showed where decades of high school students had started campfires; various names and statements were written onto the stones with pens and markers; sprayed on in every conceivable shade of Krylon; or carved into any available surface while scads of empty beer cans, liquor bottles, fast-food containers, and empty condom wrappers gave mute testimony to what the kids were doing when they weren't indulging their artistic and literary muses.

But not one sign of Mr. Johnson. I loped back to the street and walked slowly along the edge of the road, looking… got it.

Right in the middle of the lot that the sheriff had called "the old Johnson place" I found two parallel lines maybe a handspan apart, where the leaves had been moved and turned over, their damp bottoms dark in the sunlight, as if by someone walking through in a shuffle. Say, an elderly man. I knelt and brushed gently to the right of the trail and was rewarded when I came across a round impression—a little larger than a quarter—partially covered by a leaf.

"Car 12, car 10."

"Go ahead."

"I've got tracks at the old Johnson place."

"10-4."

Out of habit I stayed to the left of the tracks, but I moved quickly. The sun was going down, and night wasn't going to make this any easier. The tracks led through the brush and up onto a foundation slab, straight up the center of the slab for several yards, before making an abrupt left turn, marching off the slab, and then angling northwards of the Carter place.

Five minutes later, as the sun was going down, I found Mr. Johnson.

There was a low—no taller than the middle of my thigh— fieldstone wall separating the two lots, and sometime in the past there had been a pecan tree next to the wall.

He was sitting on top of the wall, back against the stump, his spiffy feather-adorned bowler hat a sharp contrast to his neat blue pajamas, a rusted metal box sitting in his lap and the cane leaning against the wall.

"Car 12, County. Code 4."

If one were to squint real hard, it would be easy to believe that he was lost in thought or maybe napping.

But I could tell from ten feet away that he was not.

"Car 10, car 12, do you need Rescue?"

I took my hat off and put it on the wall. Then, I stripped off my gloves and dropped them into the hat. His right hand was resting on top of the metal box, and I slipped my fingers to the inside of his wrist to check for a pulse.

Nothing.

Looped around his index finger, held in place by his thumb, was a ribbon, badly faded to a dove gray but probably once the cornflower shade that might have been used to tie back the hair of a blue-eyed blonde girl.

"Car 12?"

I gently placed my fingers on the side of his throat. He was cold, and there hadn't been a pulse there for some time.

"County to car 12."

Funny how there seemed to be a hitch in my throat. I squeezed the fragile shoulder softly and then hit the "send" button on my walkie-talkie, "County, negative on Rescue. Signal 9."

A long pause before the county dispatcher replied, "10-4, 12." She would be calling a Justice of the Peace to come to pronounce— there was going to need to be a path cleared for that and for the funeral home, but it just didn't feel right to leave that old gentleman alone again. Not in the dark.

The sheriff and the volunteer fire department would be here soon enough.

FILE 13
Napoleon Complex

There was a young man who moved to our town named Frederick who managed to get on my wrong side in a hurry.

Near as I can tell, his mama gave him anything he wanted from the time he learned to point. In her eyes, he could do absolutely no wrong.

He was, in plain language, spoiled bloody rotten. Top this with the fact that Frederick was five foot, four inches tall and the possessor of one well-fed Napoleon Complex, should enable anyone to foresee the trail of smacked-around girlfriends, lost brawls, unreturned rental movies, unpaid gasoline, burn-out marks, skipped bills, hot checks, harassing phone calls, and a record number of Public Disturbance and Disorderly Conduct calls, except, apparently, his mother. Who also moved to our fair town.

I believe he holds the record for shooting to the top of the sheriff's Smoke List.

I was patrolling the west side of town one balmy Friday night, when about 3 in the A.M., I saw headlights up the street that looked wrong.

I pulled up to the house and immediately discovered the reason the headlights looked wrong: they were coming from a car high-centered on the bank of a koi pond occupying the front lawn of a corner residence.

From the trail of brutally slaughtered garden gnomes, it appeared that the driver of the car had chosen a spot some twenty feet shy of the stop sign to make a right turn.

I parked the cruiser at the curb, turned on the lightbar, and picked my way through the gnomic massacre to the driver's side of the expensive European convertible sports car.

Since the window was rolled down, I could clearly see that the driver's seat was occupied by my favorite Frederick, who was making very careful movements of the steering wheel while peering blearily, albeit intently, through the windshield.

I cleared my throat, "Ahem. Sheriff's office."

Freddie practically jumped out of the seat, whipped around, and stared at me like a deer caught in headlights.

I waggled my fingers at him.

Freddie reached down and pushed the UP button for the driver's side window, closing the convertible's window in my face (I guess), very carefully engaged the right-hand turn signal, and gently turned the steering wheel to the right. The engine revved politely.

I stepped back and looked at the koi pond. Yep, still high-centered.

I will admit that I waited until Freddie had released a massive sigh of relief and shakily wiped his mouth before I tapped on the window glass.

I'm evil that way sometimes.

Young Freddie jumped damned near a foot out of the seat, clutched his fists to his chest, and stared at me in a mixture of absolute confusion and just a bit of panic.

I made cranking motions with my hand. Freddie continued to stare at me. Getting a little irritated, I reached over the top of the window and unlocked and opened the door. Freddie promptly scrambled into the passenger seat, curled up into a little ball, and began a loud, rapid, and totally unconvincing snoring.

I performed a Migraine Salute. Freddie peered at me through one eye and then began to snore even louder and faster. I moved the transmission into P, turned off the engine, dropped the keys into my pocket, walked around to the passenger side, and said politely, "Sheriff's office, Freddie. Step out of the vehicle, please."

To which Young Freddie yelped, "Can'tsh choo shee I'm as... asleep?! Fug, funk, [deleted] off, joo dumb [deleted]!"

I'm not exactly sure what the alcohol had been telling Freddie, but I don't think me getting a satisfying double handful of the front of his silk shirt and snatching him out the passenger seat of his car was a part of the plan.

I love convertibles.

We wound up nose to nose, his toes a good six inches off the turf, and me smiling a very large, not-very-friendly smile. "Are you awake now, Fred... Jesus, Mary, and Joseph, what the hell have you been drinking?"

"Scroo... screwd... screwdrivers, joo fug... fickin', [deleted]ing maroon, no, moron."

"Okay, Freddie, let's go over to the nice cop car."

"Whafer... wotsifor... why?"

"Because I said so, Freddie."

"Joo got gotta tell me wha's... why Ah'm bein' adrested for."

"Gnomicide and suspected DWI. You want to walk to my cruiser, or do I drag you?"

"'M gonna home. Choo... joo talk to by lagyer in... de... de morn, 'Ey! Leggo de eer! Ear! Choo gogda by eer!"

We arrived at the cruiser, and I retrieved Freddie's wallet and called dispatch to report my location and to run a 27/28 and a 29. I noticed that while I was on the radio, Freddie was sniveling into one of those new-fangled cell phones. To his lawyer, I assumed.

Hah!

I got my business done on the radio, gently inquired if Freddie wanted to perform some Standardized Field Sobriety Exercises, relieved Freddie of the phone, and repeated my inquiry about the SFSEs, to which Freddie replied loudly and profanely in the affirmative.

He then proceeded to fail the SFSEs. Spectacularly.

Which led to Freddie getting hooked up and put into the back of the cruiser. Because it was a balmy Texas night (and to give Freddie somewhere other than the floorboard to hork, when required), I compassionately left the back window down.

I had just finished telling dispatch to find a tow-truck driver with some experience at improvisation when I noticed a car hauling tail up the road toward my location. Said car screeched to a halt behind my cruiser with one tire perched comfortably on the curb, and the peroxide blonde driver exploded out and began to stomp to the cruiser. I jumped out, pointed at Freddie's mama, and firmly said, "We've had this discussion before, Darla. Remember the words 'Interfering with the Duty of an Officer'?"

"Why are you arresting my baby?!"

"Mama!"

"Oh, baby! You're in handcuffs! Why is he in handcuffs!?"

"That would be under the 'arresting' part, Darla. Driving While Intoxicated." I gestured toward the car, the koi pond, and the lawn with its pitiful population of decapitated Little Folk.

"He shaid... said I kildt a ganomey. I din't meen too, but hesh wouldn't gegt... get... off my way! I'd hoknt de horn and evvrthing! Idt washn't my fault!" bawled Freddie.

"Darla, he drove his car over that lawn. He reeks of booze, and he failed every single one of his sobriety tests. He's drunk, he was driving, and he's going to jail just as soon as the wrecker gets here."

"Bull[deleted]! My baby doesn't get drunk. Nobody can pass those [deleted]ing sobriety tests! See?" Matching actions to words, Darla flung her head back, attempted to stab herself in the eye with a polycarbonate fingernail, and tumbled against the side of my cruiser.

I immediately began to help her up, when I noticed that Darla's eyes were... awfully bloodshot. And under the pungent whiff of Chanel... was that... booze? Darla smacked my helping paw away and stood, swaying ever so gently, with her hands on her hips.

"See? My baby can't pass those tests because nobody can pass those [deleted]ing tests!"

"Yeah!" yelped Freddie.

My smile was probably beatific.

"Actually, Freddie did the tests over here in front of the cruiser, where there's light."

Darla stomped around the front of my cruiser, attempted to touch her nose, and caught herself on the hood of my car, glaring triumphantly at me.

"He also tried the walk and turn. Want me to show you how it's supposed to be done?"

"I [deleted]ing know how it's supposed to be done!" So saying, she promptly failed that one, too. An angelic choir was softly singing hosannas in my ear as I gently mentioned that Freddie had failed the Horizontal Gaze Nystagmus, and surely she...

"I bet I've got a nystagmus, too! Check and see!?"

"Yeah!" announced Freddie.

How could I say no?

When I was done with my light, Darla looked at me triumphantly, "See? What did I tell you?"

"You are totally correct, Darla," I said, feeling around for my spare set of handcuffs on the gear shift of the cruiser, "You said you'd fail the sobriety tests, and you did. Each and every one."

"So you're going to let my baby go?"

"Hell, no." I waved the handcuffs at her.

Took me five minutes to get that biting, screaming, kicking, clawing, spitting, cussing hellcat into the cruiser, I'm here to tell you.

Worth it, though.

FILE 14

City Folk

Being in an area of Texas outside the Austin city limits, we don't get a lot of protests or other bushwa of that nature. We are, however, on a route between Here and Somewhere Else, and we have the occasional person on the way to Somewhere Else wind up going afoul of local law enforcement. Like the vegetarian girl with Washington plates who cussed out a cowboy at the local diner and then spit into his basket of french fries all because he was eating a burger.

By the by, ladies, a valuable lesson was learned that day. If you're going to Say It With Saliva in Texas, make sure your boyfriend can take a whuppin'.

Anyhoo, can we possible leave our angsty little problems back at the old homestead? Please?

Once upon a time... no, wait, wrong format.

Our evening deputy was cruising the northwest section of the county when this towering pillar of black smoke sort of caught his attention.

He hared off down a farm-to-market road, found the lease that the smoke was coming from, and noticed that the gate at the cattle guard was standing wide open. He went over to the cattle guard, and then down about half a mile of badly rutted dirt/clay/gravel road, to find a yellow late-model Mustang high-centered on one of the ruts. The driver's side door was standing open, and one white male was standing behind the car, attempting to rock it off of high center.

'Bout a hundred yards down the road, there was a pump-jack totally engulfed in flames.

Deputy Frank figured that there was probably a young lady somewhere, but he really wanted this car out of the way because there were a bunch of fire trucks about to come down this road, and the local Volunteer Fire Department wasn't too particular about how they moved obstructing vehicles, so he got out of the cruiser to give the young man a hand.

The young man looked up and then promptly hauled butt into the surrounding mesquite thickets. More on this later. Heh.

Frank began inventing new swear words and stomped over to the Mustang, whereupon he Made Some Observations: A) The inside of the car reeked of gasoline; and B) there was a brand-new pack of road flares in the passenger seat; only there appeared to be one flare missing.

While we may be a Small Town, that doesn't mean that we're dumb.

Other deputy showed up, and together they got the Mustang pushed out of the way just before the fire department roared down the road and did their best with the conflagration.

Anyhoo, Himself came out and inspected the scene, and we found the back seat of the Mustang plumb buried under hand-written pamphlets, mimeographed manifestos, and other such niceties.

Seems like the lad had a case of the hips regarding "Energy conglomerates and the rape of the petrochemical wealth of the planet." Or somesuch.

The sheriff sighed and had a reserve deputy and myself sit on the hood of the Mustang in case Todd the Eco-Warrior made his way back while the on-duty deputy got to drive up and down the FM roads surrounding the lease with orders to snatch any hitchhikers.

Let me see a show of paws from the people who have experience in North Texas mesquite thickets.

snicker

Mesquites have very long thorns, and they grow very low to the ground and very close together. In addition, mesquite thickets are the favored lairs of ticks, no-see-ums, wheel bugs, tarantulas, fire ants, red ants, spiders, and pasty-faced men with chainsaws. Not to mention that cactus, jumping-getcha, devil's claw, and other antisocial plants also like thickets.

The wind doesn't ever seem to get into the mesquite thickets, but the humidity does. And the heat. And here's our critter, in his black no-dye tissue-thin batik cotton drawstring drawers and his politically correct black hemp guayabera shirt and his black cordura sandals.

Anyhoo, Bubba and I sat there juggling a can of Deep Woods Off for about twenty minutes before hearing this blood-curdling yodel, and we saw Todd the Revolutionary, black bandanna pulled up bandit-style over his lower face, burst forth from the mesquite in a buzzing gray cloud and sprint for the open driver's door of the Mustang, ululating every step of the way.

We watched him cover the hundred or so feet at a dead sprint, and then Bubba casually reached over and pushed the door closed, causing Young Toddy to ricochet off the closed door and into the dust, much to the delight of the mosquitoes.

I waved the car keys at him. I supposed I needed to read the *Anarchist Handbook* because this was apparently a gross violation of the rules of the game. All five foot, six inches, 130 pounds of halitosis and macrobiotic methane jumped to his feet, struck a bee-yoo-ti-ful tai chi stance, and proclaimed, "It took six LAPD pigs to take me to jail. I'm not afraid of you!"

snort

He went to jail.

FILE 15
No Gun

The night-shift deputy in that particular county had been in law enforcement of one kind or another since the 1960s. Listening to him talk about how Things Used To Be Done could be a bit hair raising if you were a fellow officer. If you weren't a peace officer, he'd tell Norman Rockwell stories about the Good Old Days. If you were a cop, he'd tell you how things actually were.

Folks that wax eloquent about how much better law enforcement was in the early and mid-part of the 20th century never heard that old boy talk about how the best cure for a kid giving an officer sass was a backhand to the mouth.

Eight o'clock one morning, and the night-shift deputy—a barrel-chested old man with watery blue eyes and a John Wayne drawl—had been officially off the clock for two hours. The pistol belt gets fairly heavy after a while, so he had been more than glad to take it off while he and I drank coffee and shot the bull as my shift started.

We didn't even get halfway through the first cup when dispatch got a 911 call from the Housing Complex. Seemed that Alphonse Jones was trying to kill his mama.

I was out the door, with Mr. Ned hot on my heels, jumped in the cruiser, and tore off for the scene. In the excitement, neither Mr. Ned nor I noticed that he hadn't put his gun belt back on.

We sailed into the neighborhood, and sure enough, Alphonse and his mama were rolling around in the street outside her house, slapping, hair-pulling, and screaming fit to make a sailor blush, much to the amusement of the crowd gathered around to watch the festivities.

Mr. Ned and I promptly parted the crowd and snatched up Alphonse and his mama. I had his mama over by the back bumper of the cruiser, trying to get a coherent story out of her, when I noticed that Alphonse was getting stupid with Mr. Ned.

"Alphonse," said Mr. Ned in that low, slow John Wayne voice of his, "You get over to your Granma's house. I'll talk to you in a bit."

"I'm staying right here," yelped Alphonse, "You got no right to tell me to go nowhere!"

"Alphonse," drawled Mr. Ned, "I'm telling you to get along."

About this time both Alphonse and I noticed that Mr. Ned wasn't wearing a gun belt. Alphonse had his back up, he had the crowd egging him on, and I was not seeing a Good Future for either Mr. Ned or me. I started eyeing the distance to the shotgun in the front seat.

"You ain't got no gun, Mr. Ned!" crowed Alphonse, "You ain't got no authority over here!" He started weaving in on Mr. Ned, hands not quite fisted and not quite up, but getting that way in a hurry.

"Alphonse, I'm not going to tell you again. You get in your Granma's house, and you do it now."

"You ain't got no gun!" Alphonse was crouched now, hands up and open as he shuffled toward Mr. Ned. He jerked his head a bit, feinting. There was a sudden movement, and Mr. Ned had Alphonse by the shirtfront with one hand and the other hand fisted up by Alphonse's face.

"What's that look like to you, boy?" Still low, still slow.

Alphonse's eyes crossed as he tried to focus on the Beretta Jetfire stuffed breech-deep in his left nostril. The silence from the crowd was awe inspiring—so complete that I could hear Alphonse gulp twenty feet away.

"L-l-looks like I'm g-going to Gramma's house?"

"Git."

You know, there really isn't anything you can add to that sort of thing.

FILE 16
Masterminds

"Reno" was my partner at the time. A barrel-chested fireplug, he is one of the few people I've met with a more cynical view of the world than myself. And that's saying something.

A "Lifer" isn't someone with a Life Sentence, as several of my Gentle Readers surmised. Instead, a "lifer" is someone who has been in and out of the criminal justice system for so long that he is institutionalized and really doesn't know any life other than the criminal one.

One of the things that tends to make me twitch about Hollywood is the fact that it gets "prison" and "jail" mixed up and figures that the two words are interchangeable. A "prison" and a "jail," at least in Texas, are two very, very different things.

With complete, total and abject apologies to Mister Shakespeare.

Today on *The LawDog Files* your Humble Correspondent brings two extra-special examples of the Criminal Mastermind at Work.

Ladies and gentlethings, I give you Critter #1. For simplicity sake, we'll call him "Richard."

Now, although Richard had an extensive amount of documentation as to his status as a juvenile delinquent, Richard was still fairly young. He had, to his dismay, discovered that the ability to beat his mother and various girlfriends senseless did not count for quite as much as he had thought it might here in the criminal corrections system.

Damn the luck.

So, Young Ricky had decided that he had to gain some street cred whilst in the county. He had to prove—beyond a doubt—that he was hard in order to avoid becoming someone's Bestest Buddy In The Whole Wide World, if you know what I mean and I think you do.

Somehow, Ricky had decided that he required a tattoo to properly display his chops.

The story that is being held to is that Ricky had come to this conclusion all on his ownsome. However, Reno and I were of the mindset that the sum total brainpower possessed by Richard consists of one solitary neuron weeping all alone in the empty darkness behind his eyes. In other words, Ricky had some coaching to come up with this tattoo idea all by himself.

Anyhoo, where was I? Oh, yes. Young Ricky, full of enthusiasm regarding the respect he would gain by way of this tattoo, approached one of the lifers in his tank and requested that the lifer "ink him up."

The critter meditated upon this and asked Ricky what sort of ink he wanted.

Ricky responded that he wanted a cross right in the center of his back.

Nae problemo, responds the critter, and they got right to it.

Richard thereupon spent some time being inked. There was hissing; there was gnashing of teeth; there was the plain and simple fact that Richard was getting stuck multiple times in the back by a staple that had no doubt been bled upon by every-stinking-body in that tank.

Ah well, the things we do for respect.

At last, it was done! Richard thanked the lifer, showed the tattoo to the tank, and struck a pose: there was applause!

Flushed with the happy knowledge that He Has Cred, Richard went to his cell to examine this princely work of art in the mirror.

Yet there was something... not quite right. As a matter of fact, the cross embedded in the skin of his back didn't quite look like... that was not a cross-bar... it actually looked a lot like... a cannon? Or maybe two cantaloupes in a sack, draped over a pipe?

And then the Awful Truth dawned. Rather than the cross requested, he had received a depiction of the—how can I say this—*defining anatomy* of the male of the species? In magnificent, rampant glory. In ink. On his back.

Young Richard immediately exited his cell, impugned the character of the tattoo artiste verbally and at length, and then attempted to extract recompense from the hide of the lifer.

"Attempted" being the operative word because that long-term resident of the Texas Penal System promptly proceeded to stomp a mudhole in his recent client's butt and walk it dry.

Which led to deputies breaking up the squabble with no little enthusiasm, followed shortly thereafter by the lifer, Richard, and Richard's new tattoo getting tossed bodily into solitary.

snicker

Critter #2 was a member of a criminal street gang which had been tear-arsing around the county seat, pulling drive-by shootings, a knifing or three, and stealing everything that wasn't nailed down. And, by the way, I am reliably informed that if you can pry it loose, it waren't nailed down.

Anyhoo, the locals got a bellyfull of this bushwa and proceeded to file a Gang Injunction against the most prolific of the gang, which included Critter #2.

As soon as #2 received his copy of the injunction, he decided that Da Law was keeping tabs on him, to include taps on his phone, pager and cell-phone surveillance, and so forth.

In this, he was faced with a truly troublesome dilemma: he was forbidden from associating physically with his homies, yet he wished to link up with his buddies in order to cock a snook at the judge who had issued the injunction.

How to do this without tipping off the eavesdropping fuzz? How?

By using his MySpace account, duh.

So he got onto his MySpace page, and he posted the details and waited for his posse to log on and to link up.

Huzzah!

Plans were made. Op-orders were written. Involved discussions on the best way to avoid getting nicked ensued.

And voila! They showed their defiance to the judge by taking pictures of themselves in a large group. One of them had the bright idea to write scurrilous opinions regarding the judge on a handy piece of paper and to hold it for a group photo while simultaneously giving the camera multiple International Peace Signs.

Wait! This was not good enough! How to properly chastise the judge? How?

Of course! One gang member got a copy of the paper and turned it to the headline about the injunction, and they posed for another picture, holding the paper high and proud while flashing their gang signs.

Take that, minion of the law!

And what better way to immortalize this deed of derring-do than to post the pictures on that very same MySpace page?

Yeah.

Did Critter #2 remember to make his MySpace page, not to mention the flagrant and obvious confessions to violations of the injunction, private?

What do you think?

These are the criminals I have to deal with. Where is my mastermind, dammit? Where is my Lex Luthor?

Dr. Doom wouldn't have left a confession on his public MySpace page.

sigh

Oh, well. If they were smart, I'd be out of a job.

FILE 17

Shift Summation

My friend Kelly Grayson, also known as Ambulance Driver around the Blogosphere, has been involved with the Kilted To Kick Cancer fundraisers from pretty much the very start. For those of you who don't know, Kilted To Kick Cancer is to raise awareness of male-specific cancers—prostate and testicular cancer for those of you who are less-squeamish than most—and involves those gentlemen wearing kilts when- and where-ever possible during the month of September. There is a fund drive and all of the usual. One year I was attempting to do my part and started posting end-of-shift reports I had sent from when I was assigned as a supervisor in the jail, with the caveat that if my Gentle Readers liked the reports, that they should donate something to KTKC, and I would post another report.

'Allo, 'allo.

Where to start…

Inmate J from the Swing Shift summation was still trying to get his books that the chief deputy had denied him; I imagine he'll keep trying.

River shook down West/8 and had all sorts of fun. We found a pair of sneakers in Inmate X's bunk, with no note in either his Misc Notes screen or his Medical screen; and we found a zip-lock bag of band-aids, triple antibiotic ointment, gauze, and all sorts of medical goodness where Inmate Q was bunking, but again, nothing in the Misc Notes or Medical screens, and no "May Keep In Tank" sticker on the zip-lock baggie. So, of course, we glommed onto them. After Inmate X threw a walleyed hissy-fit, I called the nurse to check. I'll be a sonovagun, both of them had medical clearance for their goodies, although it wasn't in their computer records.

Sigh. I had to remind Ms. Cleo to start taking my calls again.

In addition to the stuff above, we also found a water-bag cover hand-sewn from a sheet, a woven plastic handle for the water-bag-cover, half of a Diet Coke can, a complete Gatorade bottle, half of a Dr. Pepper can, a tattoo pick, umpteen squillion loose staples, a large garbage bag, about twenty feet of fishing cord, a fishing pole, a spare uniform, several extra linens, one of which Inmate T was sneaking in a very personal location, anatomically speaking. Yes, a whole sheet. I was impressed. And the usual flotsam and jetsam.

After the shakedown was through, as we were returning the inmates to West/8, Inmate N tried pushing Officer Oldskool's buttons. Didn't go so well for the lad, although he's got enough smarts not to go far enough to earn a Use of Force. We might keep an eye on the mouthy little squab, though.

River did water-checks at 0319.

When we checked the temps, the Special Housing Unit was showing between 85 and 86, so I bumped the thermostats down a wee bit and had the purge run. An hour later, the temperatures were around the 80-degree mark.

Over at Central, the kitchen lost power about 0045-ish and got it back somewhere around 0245. Then, it went out again at 0436, came back, went out again at 0447, and came back about 0500. We were feeding bag meals to the inmates for breakfast.

Central/North did water-checks at 0458 and shook-down Central/North/1, finding a candle and a tattoo pick.

Central/Female checked their water at 0453.

In other news, Eduardo was proving to be a slipperier character than I had thought. He does remain unflushed at this time. Thing 1 gently requested that he be evicted from the control room before her next tour, which I believe to be this Sunday.

Personally, I was giving hard thought to handing the little bugger a radio and assigning him to the West Tier.

That should be about it.

Nothing but (appropriate) love,

LawDog, NCOIC
Bugscuffle SO

FILE 18
Kerfuffle in West/8

The shift summations were an immediate hit, although several Gentle Readers thought I must be exaggerating the actual reports. Nope. Other than anonymizing people, these are the word-for-word reports I used to send out.

The reason that these reports were written in such an over the top manner is that I hate being required to do something that everyone is going to ignore. If I was going to be forced to write a shift summation, then, by God, people weren't going to ignore it.

We shifted report systems some time later, and I stopped having to do the reports. This was apparently met with much dismay from people who had gotten into the habit of reading my 0600 reports over breakfast.

Good morning, ladles and germs,

To start out our night at River properly, Inmate B decided to play possum after headcounts. He refused to stir for officer shouts and banging on the door, and when we went into SHU/23, he didn't respond to shaking, tapping, or sweet nothings bellowed into his ear. I was trying to decide if I could creatively articulate getting a response with a drive-stun when, apparently, his telepathy decided to kick in, and he said Bad Things to us. Which was good enough evidence of being alive in my book.

River did water-checks at 0256 and shook-down East/3. We came up empty handed, which, considering that our inmates were not that well-behaved, made me wonder what new hiding place they were hiding their stuff in these days.

Central/North did their water-checks at 0106 and Central/Female at 0103. Central/Female also shook-down Female/9 and came up with several extra blankets. However, they also reported that while the trusties were in the visitation area during the shakedown, two of them got into each other's faces. Seems like all was not happy in Trustieland.

Tonight's medal-winner in the D'oh! Contest was Inmate G in Intake. By all accounts the wee lass got nicked by PD for DWI, was delivered into our tender custody, and wound up in Detox/2 for Grand Mopery and Contempt of Cop (misdemeanor). Once there, she proceeded to throw one bee-yoo-ti-ful walleyed, ringtail temper tantrum. As uncle to several sprogs betwixt the ages of two and nine, I can recognize true artistry in fit throwing, and this was One Of A Kind.

She screamed, hollered, beat on the bench, spun in circles on the floor, kicked the door, all the usual, but what elevated this performance to High Art was when she took off her jeans and used them to beat the unoffending cell camera until the picture fuzzed.

The intake crew, being the unappreciative Philistines that they were, took a dim view of this display and chained her drunk butt to the bench. One would have thought that this would have been the curtain call, but our Intrepid Damsel proceeded to take off her shirt and strangle her-own-self with it. Which got her stripped nekkid and placed on Suicide Watch as well as being chained to the bench. Goodness, I hope that was all worth it.

As I wrote this, we had some kind of kerfuffle in West/8.

Inmate M decided to remove himself from West/8. According to Inmate M, Inmate J sent another inmate to Inmate M to inform Inmate M that Inmate J did not want him in "his" tank. Goodness. 'Twere I a betting man, I'd lay money that the inmate delivering the message was going to be Inmate T. I may have made a strategic error in moving those two from Central/North/6 a while back. Anyhoo, Inmate M was moved to West/1, and when I got back to River tonight, I planned to separate Inmates J and T; with a Separation Notation in both their records. And depending on my mood, I was liable to see how far I could spread the inhabitants of West/8 around.

In other news, I discovered that a field mouse had taken up residence in the River control room. The kids named it Eduardo. While intriguing, I scotched the suggestion that Eduardo be sponsored through the Basic County Corrections Course; and as soon as I became able to snag his little butt, Eduardo would probably be taking a "vacation" by way of the Porcelain Express.

Hmm. That's about it, I think.

In closing,

LawDog, NCOIC
Bugscuffle SO

FILE 19

Contraband

I'm given to understand that the throw-away joke regarding Mrs Lincoln got someone's nose out of joint, but apparently it tickled the sheriff so much that nothing came my way about it.

Hullo,

It was one fun evening out here at River. Right off the bat Inmate S in West/3 came up with a jolly huge rash and stated he was starting to have problems breathing. Nurse came out, did some nursing-type stuff, and watched him for a bit. He seemed to get better.

Right after that, Inmate M and Inmate Y got into a fight in West/4. Review of the video shows that while it may have been mutual combat, Inmate Y instigated it. Both got disciplinary cases and were moved to other tanks. Then, Inmate R in West/4 started yelping about having something in his eye. We told the nurse, and he said to tell Inmate R to flush the eye with water and to try to go to sleep.

Officer Slowyerroll has the sort of radio voice that would accompany a gentle pat on the shoulder and the words, "Other than that,

Mrs. Lincoln, how was the play?" so when he laconically asked if a supervisor could come back to SHU/19, I started grabbing every party favor I could find and hit the control room door at a high lope. Sure enough, Inmate Q had taken both covers off the power outlet in that cell and was into the wiring up to his knuckles. I'm here to tell you that it kind of made pointing the Taser at him a bit… superfluous. We settled for snatching his butt off the table and scooting him down to SHU/5, which had no interior power outlets for him to muck about with.

Of course, Inmate K was the occupant of SHU/5, and of course, he had to be difficult about giving up his cell. Diplomacy won the day as Inmates K and Q swapped cells with only minor grumbling.

I was feeling my oats a bit at that time, so I had officers tell East/3—on the down-low—that they were catching a shakedown, but if they threw out their contraband, the officers would try to talk me into leaving their colored boxers in the tank. Last I checked, the hallway in front of East/3 was ankle deep, and folks in East/3 were offering to trade commissary to East/4 in return for more stuff they could throw out.

While East/3 was unloading their contraband, we hit the kitchen and the laundry. Came up with five chicken quarters, two sandwiches, and two Styrofoam cups of sugar hidden in various places. Then, we started on the SHU cells, beginning with Inmate C in SHU/16 since he had a fresh tattoo. When we woke him up, he was wearing a set of white boxers on over a set of colored ones, and he got kittenish about giving up the colored ones. I said not to mind, put him in the hall, and started searching his cell. Good lord. We got string, a magnet, string, four sparkers, string, and I'm pretty sure we accidentally dropped his tat pick into the light fixture trying to get it out. Then, we brought him back in, explained that the white underwear made his colored underwear contraband, and might we please have it?

Inmate C was a bit of an oik. He got a case of the arse and told us we weren't getting the underwear. Then, he offered to give us a proper thumping if we tried. I demurred and said that I wasn't leaving the cell without the contraband, and Inmate C told me to go get rank. I checked my sleeves to see if I had remembered to put on my stripes, and Inmate C sneered for me to go get "real rank." Further declared that we would have to go get the sheriff and that if the sheriff came out right then and right there and told him to give up the underoos, then—and only then—would he give them up.

We got the boxers. Since he had more fishing line, a bit of paper folded into a weight, and two notes to and from Inmate F, who was at that time two doors down from Inmate C's solitary cell, tucked into the front of his boxers. I guessed that was why he was such a numpty about giving them up. I went ahead and photocopied the page of the Inmate Handbook regarding colored and white underwear and attached it to the grievance he was demanding.

River did water and intercom checks at 0339; Central/North did theirs at 0005 and Central/Female at 0158. Central/North also did the needful and shook North/7. Officers advised that they found the burned stubs of jailhouse cigarettes, but that was about all.

Spreading peace and joy, I remain:

LawDog, NCOIC
Bugscuffle SO

FILE 20

A Memory I Will Treasure Always

When I was writing these Shift Reports, I had been reassigned to the jail and was working the midnight shift. Working deep mids gives you plenty of time to think, and, being of a philosophical nature, and having found a metric butt-ton of shanks in a couple of shakedowns, I started thinking.

The Bugscuffle County Jail—and other similar facilities around the State of Texas and the United States as a whole—is pretty much just as close to the liberal dream of a total gun-control Utopia as you can get.

No guns allowed, ever. No guns, no knives, no weapons. Not on the officers, not on the inmates. Full gun control. Period. Full stop. End of story.

Granted, the Bugscuffle County Jail Special Housing Unit isn't the gun control Mecca that, say, San Quentin or Pelican Island are, but one of my officers did get stabbed, non-fatally, with a golf pencil by an inmate at SHU some time ago.

He was stabbed by this inmate, as a point of fact, because he was "the kindest officer" on shift that day. My paw to Freyja, that quote is the absolute truth.

Alternatively, an hour or so in a 40-man Max pod could be instructive. Again, while our Max pods have the same stringent gun control as Attica Correctional or Angola, we're not quite the Gun Control Paradise those places are. Only a handful or so of our inmates have needed medical care after inmate-on-inmate violence. This year.

So, I have to ask: if gun control is the panacea these folks think it is, why aren't they clocking in to the safety, peace, and quiet of a boring shift at Sing-Sing or ADX Florence? Complete and total gun control means those should be amongst the safest places in the world, right?

Dear ladles and germs,

To start off the night on a high note, we had water falling from the skies. I had heard the Old Ones speak of such a thing from days past, but I had never thought to see it with my own eyes.

There were no leaks reported either at River or Central.

Officers spotted Inmate C passing something from East/5 to Inmates R and F in East/4. Suspecting tobacco, we hit the tank, but Inmates F and R got to the khazi before we did. We shook East/4 anyway and came up aces when we found a bee-yoo-ti-ful tattoo pick in R's property and a baggie of ink in the general area. To show my appreciation, we moved Inmate R to West/2 pending a disciplinary case for Possession of Tattoo Paraphernalia, shifted Inmate C one tank further along to East/6, and left Inmate F in East/4.

Tier scuttlebutt has it that Inmates R, C, and F were getting tobacco from Inmate F2 in East/1.

While we were shaking down East/4, officers spotted West/1 working out with a water bag, but they had an attack of the dumbs and denied having the contraband. Since I had a surfeit of knuckle-draggers handy, we overrode the doors in West/1 and retrieved the water bag. The startled faces in that tank were a memory that I will treasure always.

Inmate H in SHU/6 got kittenish about chaining up for cell cleaning. I went down, and he decided to comply, but when it came time to remove the restraints, he decided to grab an officer's hand and squeezed as hard as possible. That went about as well as might be expected. Then, he took out his frustration on the door to SHU/6, and I am told that the door to SHU/6 oft comes agley when beaten upon. Sigh. So we went back and took him to SHU/10. Surprisingly enough, he went meek as a lamb.

Of course, a scant breath after getting Inmate H relocated, Inmate R (from the tobacco and My First Tattoo Kit incident in East/4) told officers that if we didn't move him to a solitary cell, he would hurt himself. Despite multiple inmates advising that this was not the course of action he really wanted, Inmate R decided to insist that he would do himself an injury if we didn't oblige him with a solitary cell. Okay. From the look on his face, I thought that the suicide smock was a wee touch drafty.

The low West tanks started getting annoying about the recent trend of seizing their colored knickers and accused us of making rules up. I gave them the page number in the Inmate Handbook so they could read it for themselves, but it turns out that none of the low West tanks had any Inmate Handbooks. I printed up one for each of the low West tanks, and—rather kindly, I think—pointed out the page that stated that destroying the Inmate Handbook would result in the tank TeeVee being turned off for "an indeterminate time." They got real quiet and stayed that way.

Officer H managed to reopen a cut on her lip from earlier that bled like God's own water faucet. We tried to get her to blame an inmate, but she wouldn't follow through. Sigh. The nurse came out and got the bleeding stopped.

Once that was done, Officer R sprinted through the River Control Room with his face a most unbecoming shade of green. Seemed the lad had eaten something that didn't agree with him because he spent about ten minutes praying to the porcelain throne. After happily advising him to check for toenails and suggesting that he swallow hard if he felt something round and furry coming up, I told him he could go home. I am here to report that Officer R was a trooper and stayed.

Intake reported that "Inmate M came back from the hospital at 0500."

River did water and intercom checks at 0311; Central/North did theirs at 0151 and Central/Female at 0112. Center/North also reported shaking down North/8 and North/4 but not finding anything of interest.

LawDog, NCOIC
Bugscuffle SO

FILE 21
The Monster Inside

Each of us has a monster down deep inside.

It's made of fangs, talons, and shadow, and it glories in blood, fire, and pain.

It's been a part of us since before we climbed down out of the trees, wrapped around our hind brains; it is there today, and it will be there as long as humans are human.

It is, after all, one of those things that makes humans human.

Some will argue that it is our intelligence that makes us human. Well, no doubt. Others will point out opposable thumbs, and they probably have a point.

However, Gentle Reader, I put it to you that the ability to take a bit of rock, a stick, and some vine and to see what it may become in our minds is no more important than that monster lurking in our bones and blood.

Yes, to take those items and to turn them into a spear is important, but what use is the spear without being able to walk up and stick it into the cave bear or lion or raiding Neanderthal or any of the thousands upon thousands of other bogeymen waiting to make early H. Sapiens into a brief diorama in some other species' Museum of Natural History?

Opposable thumbs enable us—as a species—to write sonnets, turn gears, build wondrous structures, sow, weave, paint, and do everything else that makes us... us.

Before that, though, the monsters that live inside us used those thumbs to pick up stone axes, to walk into caves, and to Put Out The Cat so that our mates and our progeny could not only live but thrive without becoming Kitty Kibbles.

It's there. That monster is in good people, bad people, smart people, stupid people, big people, little people, brave ones, and cowards. If you are human, it's there.

Part of walking the warrior path involves reaching inside, grabbing your monster, and hauling it out to take a good, hard look at it because denial doesn't make your monster go away. Denial only ensures that if your monster ever does try to slip its chain, you'll not know what to do about it or even what it is.

That's the thing: those people who swear they don't have a monster—when theirs gets loose, they don't have a clue. Their monster runs them, and that's a recipe for an unpleasantness.

Man should always control his monster. It's when the monster controls man that things get nasty. And you can't control your monster with denial or ignorance.

You can't control your monster unless you know it. Unless you know what it looks like, what it feels like, what it feeds off... and what it can do.

I once engaged in a debate with a young lass who swore that my assertions regarding the monster that lives in each of us were totally mistaken. Not everyone, said she, had a monster. Surely I didn't think that she had a monster.

In response I asked if she had a child or if there was a young child in her immediate family. There, indeed, was. A niece, of whom she was very fond. I then asked her to engage in a creative articulation with me. I asked her to imagine that she and her niece were in a room and that the room was empty of everything except one other person.

She said that she could, and then I told her that the other person was Jeffrey Dahmer.

There was a long pause, and then she stated that she'd obviously call the police. I responded that Jeffrey Dahmer was bigger than she was, stronger, faster—and, of course, a serial killer.

I asked her how much she cared for her niece, and then I mentioned that there was a hammer in the room and asked her to think honestly about her response.

She looked at me for a long time, and then I said, "Hey, look. Monster."

When she told me to go to Hell, I figured that I had gotten my point across.

Today, we had a young man come to jail for burglary. Not only was he a long-term substance abuser, but he had almost mechanically perfect scars up the inside of both forearms from wrist to elbow.

I spoke to him gently. He was obviously still under the effect of whatever the current recreational pharmaceutical du jour is but was coherent enough to assure me that he had thrown away any blade that he had kept around for the purpose of cutting himself. He told me several times that he wasn't stupid enough to keep a weapon about his person while committing a burglary and seemed somewhat aggrieved that I would ask him such a thing.

When the razor blade used by a self-mutilating, substance-abusing critter to carve multiple dozens of lacerations into the flesh of both his forearms slid through my nitrile glove and several millimeters into my right index finger, I knew exactly what that electric burn meant.

My monster roared up out of my hind brain, fueled by such things as "HIV," "Hepatitis," and "LIAR," and for a brief instant my monster filled my mind with visions of rage and blood, of crushing fury and punishing pain.

Only for that briefest of instants, though.

I ordered the critter not to move, informed the other officers that I'd been injured by a blade in his pocket, waited until they had secured the blade, and walked to the nurse's station, blood dripping off my finger every step of the way.

Later, the arresting officer sought me out to apologize for missing the razor blade in the critter's pocket during his frisk and stated, "Man, I don't know how you did it. If that would have been me stuck by that nasty razor, I would have smashed him!"

Kid, I'm a man. I control my monster—always. My monster doesn't control me—ever. Period. Full stop. End of story.

And that's something you might just want to think long and hard about.

FILE 22

Detoxification

Your Humble Scribe and a Minion were watching an inmate who was praying vigorously to Ralph, Ye Ancient God of the Porcelain Throne.

Inmate: "Oh, Gaaaawwwwd!"

"Sweet Jeebus," sayeth the Minion, looking a little greenish herself, "Does he have anything left?"

I attempted to look properly concerned but probably failed miserably, "Probably not. Pretty sure I saw toenails come out just a second ago."

"Do we need to send him to the hospital or something?" asked the Minion, who hadn't quite reached the fullness of cynicism enjoyed by her elders.

"Nah. When he was arrested—curled up under the dining room table of a complete and total stranger at three in the morning, I might add—he had a baggie with trace amounts of heroin in it. Trust me. The jail nurses are quite familiar with the protocols for opiate detox."

"You don't unnerstand!" He gulped a couple of times, "Gawd, please kill me!"

"If I were you, I'd shut up and concentrate on keeping your organs on the inside."

"Don't make fun of me! Yeeaaarrgghh!"

"If you feel something round and furry coming up, best swallow hard 'cause you're going to need it later."

Minion: "Eww."

"You're makin' fun of me!" There was a pause as he performed the old Better-Out-Than-In ritual, "I'm somebody! I went to Local State University!"

"Graduated," I snarked, feeling really proud of myself, "Magna cum laudanum, no doubt."

Inmate: "Yeah! Blargh!"

Minion (Rolling her eyes at her Mentor in All Things Knuckle-dragging): "That... was terrible."

LawDog: "I'll say. I'm pretty sure the jail kitchen doesn't serve a damn thing that color."

Minion: "Smartass."

Ah, well. The finer points of extemporaneous wit are lost on the young.

sigh

I'm so unappreciated in my time.

FILE 23

Rivers of Ink

Why a fountain pen?

Well, I'd be lying if I said that ego didn't have something to with my choice of writing instrument. People will stop what they are doing when you uncap a fountain pen and watch in fascination as you write with it.

And in today's world of mass-produced ballpoint pens and gel inks, there is something satisfying to the soul to be found in writing with an instrument which dates to the 1850s and can trace its direct lineage back to the 10th century.

The big plus to a fountain pen is the simple fact that it is easier to write with one. Fountain pen ink is liquid and flows freely. The scribe need only guide the nib across the paper, and the ink will apply itself.

Ballpoint pens, on the other paw, use paste ink and require the writer to firmly apply enough pressure to rotate the ball, dragging the paste out of the reservoir and onto the surface of the paper.

Granted, it is not a lot of pressure, but it does add up over the course of a day. Since I initial or sign over a hundred documents in a shift, answer a score or more Inmate Request Forms, Grievances, and the occasional Citizen Complaint, and annotate or add suggestions to a double handful of stuff written by other officers, my writing hand gets a bit of a workout.

It may just be my imagination, but at the end of the day I can tell
a palpable difference between a shift using a fountain pen and a shift
using a ballpoint pen.
And I just like them.

I carry two pens at work. One of which is a fine-point gel
rollerball for the frequent occasions when I'm writing or signing
something that has carbons.

The other is a fountain pen with a medium nib. This is the pen
that I use for everything else and is the one I use the most. I use it
to the point where I have to refill the converter about every three
days or so.

Somebody forgot to remind me that a promotion comes with
an exponentially expanding increase in paperwork. The bastards.

Anyhoo, part of the reason I was going through rivers of ink
was that when an Inmate Request Form, colloquially referred to
as a "kite", crosses my desk, I answer it properly.

Instead of scrawling a single word such as "Approved," "Denied," "No," or the like, I address the response to "Mr. (or Ms.)
[Insert Critter's Name Here] and write a—usually—short paragraph explaining why I am not going to authorize the inmate to
receive a My First Meth Lab in the mail or opining that if Ms.
Critter didn't want to get stripped and placed on Suicide Watch
in Solitary, then she shouldn't have tried to hang herself with a
bed sheet on video.

I hadn't realized that this would get as... distinctive... as it had,
until the other day, when an officer brought me a kite from an
inmate in the last ten minutes of my shift. It had been a long shift,

I was tired, out of ink, out of sorts, and running low on patience, and the request was a calculated attempt to game the system.

So I grabbed the kite and my rollerball, wrote a quick "Denied, see Inmate Handbook," signed it, and handed it back to the officer for return.

Lord have mercy.

I got back to work next shift, and the first thing I heard was that a certain inmate had twisted off. He was raising hell, flooded his cell, filing grievance after grievance, and generally acting the ass.

Huh. I trundled back to Solitary to ask him just what the hell his major malfunction was and to impress upon him the advantages of a nice, quiet night when, upon seeing me, he practically burst into tears.

"Mr 'Dawg! They's fraudulating a superior officer! They can't do that!"

I blinked, feeling my eyebrow slide up, and the Smartarse Gnome took the opportunity to grab my tongue. "I'm pretty sure that fraudulating violates the laws of physics, if not the laws of the State of Texas, Anthony, but which particular case of flagrant fraudulating are you referring to?"

He waved a stack of kite forms in my general direction for emphasis. "You, Mr 'Dawg! They is impressonating and fraudulating you! And I won't stands for it!"

I looked at the oncoming tier officer, "I am? Why was I not told? Did I at least hold out for dinner?" That worthy gave a puzzled shrug, which, come to think of it, is a normal response from my minions, and I turned back to the passionately declaiming Anthony.

He promptly shoved a stack of kite forms into my paws, each one with a paragraph or three on the back in rich burgundy from a medium nib. "That's you."

"Okay."

He waved a single sheet of paper upon which four words were written with a fine-nibbed blue-ink G2.

Oops.

"They said this is you, but I know better! I know better! I knows your writing, and this ain't it! They wrote it and said it was you! That's fraudulating! If someone writes something and says that someone else writes it, and that someone didn't write it, and that someone is a superior officer, that's impressonating a superior officer! I won't stands for it! It's fraudulating!"

Crap.

Why me?

FILE 24

The Power of Paper

While this isn't a funny tale, it was one of those things that I sat down at my desk and pounded out in one short stretch and turned out to be one of the more quoted things I've ever done.

I think it's even more relevant today.

I'm fond of paper.

A single sheet of paper can hold ideas, hopes, dreams; it can carry a song, orders, love; it can recall history, bear witness when none is left, and it can serve as the base of art for bairns as well as their great-grandsires.

Many folks name the invention of the printing press as a foundation stone of human civilization, but what is the use of a printing press with no paper to work with?

For all of its utility and history, though, there is one area in which paper is sorely lacking:

It makes lousy armour.

Oh, I'm sure there are fantastic suits of papier-mâché hauberks using fabled Oriental Death Bamboo paper and sacred Tibetan yak lacquer, but let us cast our gaze upon a single sheet of 8 1/2 by 11 paper.

Let us further stipulate that it is of a good, heavy kind of paper—quality stuff—say, 32lb paper. Pretty, is it not?

We shall hang this sheet of paper from something. A clothesline, maybe, or a door frame. Something that will hold the paper at the top and at the bottom yet allow some room behind the paper.

Now, flick a hand at the paper and see how much force it takes to tear through it. A simple pass of the fingers, I'd wager. Nothing as vigorous as a baseball bat, or a fireplace poker, surely.

If you were to lay a similar sheet of paper—flat, as it is meant to be read—upon someone's cheek and then slapped that cheek with all of your strength... would it absorb the blow? Would an 8.5x11 inch sheet of paper cause the impact to hurt less?

How about a punch? Would a sheet of paper—or two sheets, or three—laid upon your stomach turn the trauma of a punch? A kick?

Does anyone think a sheet of paper will stop a kitchen knife or a bullet?

No?

Let us change the exercise a bit. Take a new sheet of paper and then rummage around and find your favorite pen. With this most wonderful of writing instruments, I want you to write two words upon the pristine white surface of this sheet of paper.

The first word shall be "RESTRAINING," and just below that, write the word "ORDER." Just those two words. If those two words are not to your liking, you may substitute the words "PEACE" and "BOND," the former above the latter.

As you admire your penmanship, I urge you to contemplate how much those two words change the ability of that sheet of paper to stop slaps. To absorb punches. If this single sheet of paper was held in front of your stomach, would it stop a kick?

Not so much?

Take this sheet of paper and add columns of section signs (§) here and there, write "IN THE NAME OF THE STATE OF TEXAS" at the top and scribble a judge's name somewhere near the bottom.

How about now? Has the paper now suddenly become magical? Will you now trust this sheet of paper to stop a baseball bat aimed for your face because it has writing upon it?

sigh

Paper makes rotten armor, no matter how many inked symbols it holds.

And when it comes down to you and a critter in a deserted parking lot in the afternoon, or a busy office at brunch, or your living room at midnight at bad-breath distances, that's all your ex parte restraint order, or your peace bond, or even your Protective Order is. It is merely a piece of paper.

Oh, I hear you now: "LawDog, if I have a valid Protective Order, and the critter violates it, he goes to jail!"

Yes. He does. Remember, however, that when he does that violating, you have to be able to contact the men with guns to come help you. And then they have to come to you from wherever they are at the time you call. Until they get there, if the only thing you've got is that piece of paper.

And, as we've seen, paper just doesn't make decent armor at all.

Gentle Readers, nothing says, "Protected," quite like a Protective Order in one paw backed up by a self-defense tool in your other, and the mindset and willingness to use it behind your eyes.

FILE 25

Unhappy Meal

Yes, I once bought an inmate a Happy Meal from McDonald's. Truth be told, up until that time, no inmate that I transported had ever complained about getting a burger and fries from Micky D's before. I figured that anyone who had been in our jail for an extended period and was on the way to prison—probably for an extended period— would be happy to get some "real" food. And by "real," I mean non-institution food.

Ick.

TDC in this story refers to the Texas Department of Corrections, which is incorrect, since the proper title has been Texas Department of Criminal Justice for some time, but when I started it was always called TDC, and I'm nothing if not a man of habit.

There I was, staggering through the briefing room in search of a coffee pot when the sheriff laid a fatherly arm across my shoulders.

"'Dog," sayeth that worthy, "I just received a grievance from TDC."

I blinked at him, muzzily.

"Seems like one of our prison-bound inmates has complained that the deputy who transported him to durance vile provided him with an actual child's Happy Meal from McDonald's for lunch on said trip."

I could smell coffee. It was here. Somewhere.

"According to the inmate, when he protested, this deputy confiscated the toy from said Happy Meal, hooked it into the partition between the seats, and—I am quoting here—'Made it talk smack,' unquote, to the inmate for the rest of the trip."

Coffee. Coffeecoffeecoffee.

"In a high, squeaky voice."

Where was that little caffeine jolt of life?

"The worst of it all, according to the inmate, was the toy staring at him for the next six hours. You wouldn't happen to know if any of our officers might be inclined to do something like this, would you?"

Oh, holy days! The warrants crew had brought coffee! May flights of angels sing thee to thy rest! Coffeecoffeecoffee!

"Yeah, I didn't think so."

"Huh?" I responded, wittily, as the Blessed Java Bean of Wakefulness started firing up the old synapses.

"Nothing, 'Dog. Check with Range about firearm re-qual next week."

Hmpf.

FILE 26

Dinosaur

As I get further toward retirement age, the kids just get younger and younger, and I find I have less and less in common with them.

I don't think, however, that this makes me a member of an extinct species.

"We," announced Faithful Minion #1 with a certain amount of relish, "Have A Problem."

I looked up from the pile of paperwork that seemed to have adopted my desk as its ancestral breeding ground to see a young lady at the intake desk. Short, nervous—not unexpected considering she was under arrest for something—maybe 80 pounds.

I looked back to where someone had sent me a request for permission to look for mop handles, "Call the kitchen. Get her a sandwich." Someone needed my okay to look for bloody mop handles? Seriously?

"Ah, boss, she's deaf."

"Okay. Give her her cell phone. Let her send a reasonable number of texts."

An inmate had sent me a request for information on getting a divorce while in jail. "Didn't I just sign off on a proxy for this one to get married?!"

"PD seized her cellphone. I really think we need a dinosaur."

Huh? I looked back out to the intake desk, where the Wee Lass was poking a finger at some equipment with a puzzled air.

Ah.

I hied myself from the desk and wandered out to where our 18-to-22-year-old guest was looking from Faithful Minion #2 to the Brand-New, Just Purchased At No Small Expense 1973-era TDD machine that had been plunked down in front of her.

"This," I announced to my faithful minions in tones that emphatically did not resemble in any way, despite slanderous assertions by folks higher in rank than I, a Tyrannosaurus delivering the lecture 'Mammals: An Evolutionary Failure', "is what the deaf used to use for communication in the days before texting and email."

So saying, I dialed the number in front of the Wee Lass and placed the phone handset in the TDD cradle with a flourish.

"Ohhh," sayeth the faithful minions.

There was a long pause. A really long pause. The Wee Lass poked the TDD with a suspicious, and more than slightly uncertain, index finger. A faithful minion cleared her throat.

"Sooo… she types into the… PBB… and it talks to whoever is on the other end?"

"TDD. No. She types into the TDD here, and the message comes up on the TDD on the other end."

"Oh."

I realized what was coming just before my faithful minion opined. "Since she doesn't seem to know what the hell that PBB is, the chances of there being another one on the other end of this call—"

I raised my hand, sighed the sigh of a man beset by the inequities of dealing with young people—children, really—and asked, "How have you been communicating with her?"

"Oh, she reads lips."

Good. I turned to the Wee Lass and, enunciating fully, I asked, "Is there another number you would like us to call for you?"

The Wee Lass stared at me with one eyebrow cocked. There was another long pause, broken by Faithful Minion #2 announcing, "She reads lips. I don't think she reads mustache."

I felt my eye twitch as Faithful Minion #1 mused, "I think she can read mustaches. It's just that the mustache was saying, 'In his house at R'lyeh, dead Cthulhu lies dreaming.' Or something."

I pivoted to look at my faithful minions. Innocent faces, the lot of the little buggers.

Sigh.

FILE 27

Treed

There are two kinds of people who read this story: the kind that have dealt with a Texas feral hog in the past and read along nodding their heads and those who haven't dealt with them and think this is stretching the truth all out of sorts.

Back in the late 90s, I was on my first night patrol after having just gotten back from a gun class out of state. Along about 0500 dispatch called, "Dispatch, Car 12."

The 0500 calls are always interesting, so I admit to some anticipation, "Go ahead."

"1100 Possum Drive, 911 call, report of a possible prowler."

I sighed. 1100 Possum Drive was a nice, middle-aged lady divorcee who called in a prowler about three times a week. Said prowler always being brush rubbing the siding on her house, or a cat, or the wind.

"10-4, en route."

I pulled up in front of the residence, and I could see the Reporting Party in the bay window, still clutching her cordless phone, and pointing frantically to the back of the house.

I admit to a well-concealed sigh, waved at her, and then began making my way around the outside of the house, no doubt to spend several minutes peering into the dark.

Imagine my surprise when I turned the back corner into the backyard and came nose to snout with a bloody huge feral hog. I remember well, in the middle of that startle-response adrenaline dump, seeing the bristles fly up on his chest. Kind of like he had just gotten center punched with a Winchester 127-grain +P+ 9mm. Like the kind I carried in my P7.

And I realized that I was standing in a textbook perfect speed-rock position.

I had just enough time to mentally pat myself on the back, and then the hog, metaphorically speaking, looked down at the hole in his chest, said, again, metaphorically speaking, "Oh, you [deleted]," and then headed my way with the obvious intention of adjusting my buttock-to-shoulder-blade ratio.

Not being entirely gormless, my body, no longer admiring the shot that started this whole episode spun, took two steps, and flung me at the lower limbs of the nearest mesquite tree... about those two steps ahead of the enraged pig.

So. There I was, hanging like a panicked sloth from the lower limbs by one ankle, one hand, and one wrist while a Paleolithic-class hog stood below, loudly opining as to my ancestry and sexual proclivities and daring me to come down.

Yeah, that wasn't happening. Unfortunately, my current suspended position meant I couldn't get another shot off at the hog without winding up down on terra firma with said ambulatory chop and with him at a decided advantage.

Worse, during the mad sprint for the tree, I seemed to have dropped my walkie-talkie.

I resigned myself to not going anywhere for a while. A sentiment obviously shared by Senor Puerco.

A lot longer later than I felt was absolutely necessary, I heard the sound of a DPS cruiser pull up outside. At last, think I, backup. And not before time.

Indeed, backup soon showed itself cautiously around the corner in the form of the DPS trooper assigned to our wee town. He scanned the backyard with his flashlight—passing over me the first time, I might add—before the beam settled on the hog. It then panned up.

There were snorting noises that I suspect may have been an attempt to conceal mirth. Not a very good attempt, but at least he tried.

"Shot the hog, didn't you?"

I snarled something that may have been less than courteous, but I plead long-term discomfort.

"I told you that dinky little 9mm wasn't any good, didn't I?"

I was attempting some form of comeback when I heard the bark of a Texas DPS-issued Sig P220, and the .45 ACP round smacked the hog right behind the foreleg.

I knew this because I had a unique perspective on the second bristle spray of the morning. Which led the hog to announce, at the top of his porcine lungs, "You want a piece of me, too?"

And I watched the DPS trooper scramble to the top of an ancient outhouse with the alacrity and grace of a scalded-arsed ape.

"Nice shot, Tex" I snarked from the comfort of my mesquite tree.

"Damn," replied that worthy, "That's a big hog."

I casted a sneer in his general direction, "Why don't you thump it a couple of more times?"

Long pause.

"Can't."

"Well," I snarled, twisting a bit, "I not in any position to do anything about this, so it's pretty much up to you."

The hog sent a grunt my way, letting me know I hadn't been forgotten.

This pause was longer. Oh, for the love of... "You dropped your bangstick, didn't you?"

"I had something on my mind!" There was another pause, contemplative this time. "I've got my .32 backup."

I could feel a facial tic developing.

This went on until the sun rose, the hog trotted off with a firmly cocked snook in our general direction, and the trooper and I climbed down and solemnly swore never to speak of this again.

Fast-forward about a year, and I was in dispatch when the local game warden staggered in and headed for the coffee pot with the same sort of intensity that a man three days under the Sahara sun heads for an oasis.

"You okay, Harry? I asked, slightly concerned.

"[Deleted] monster hog out by the T bar S," he muttered from around a soothing mug, "Took three rounds from my .450 Marlin. Didn't think the [deleted] was ever going to go down."

I was mildly impressed. "Damn."

"Checked him over and found this under the skin on his chest." He displayed a perfectly mushroomed Winchester Ranger bullet. Probably about 127 grains, were I to guess, "Some damnfool moron shot him with a 9mm sometime. Can you imagine that? Idiot. Some people shouldn't be let out without a minder."

Whoops.

FILE 28
A Lesson in Respect

When I wrote this, a Gentle Reader asked if my math was on. He had apparently added the age of the gentleman in this story, subtracted some history, and was missing a decade or two.

This incident actually happened back in the 1990s.

I did get a couple of outraged emails from folks wanting to know why I just stood by while Waldo adjusted the headspace and timing on the mouthy kid. I gently replied that they probably didn't realize how fast that sort of thing can happen, how long it takes to open a security door, and how many people in the cell were going to lie to me about what had happened when we did get the door open.

He was fine. Educational beatdowns are a fact of life inside.

The intake officer gave me a call from the intake section, and I scooted on over there.

Seemed an elderly gentleman had arrived at our jail by way of the local municipal court. 80 years old, plus or minus, with exactly zero criminal or traffic records of any kind.

I looked at this gentleman—eyes clear, back straight, looking around with mild amusement—and I asked what brought him to us. Surely community service would be a better way of dealing with him?

The old gentleman fixed me with a gray eye, and in a slow drawl he said, "Son, I spent 1951 to 1953 in Korea, trying not to get my boys killed. I figure that there makes me a man grown."

I nodded, cautiously, not exactly sure where this was going.

"Now I figure that since I am a full-grown adult, and I know the risks, whether or not I wear a seatbelt isn't the business of a bunch of panty-waisted jackasses down in Austin."

Oh.

"My wife asks me to wear the damned thing, I wear it. I'm her business. My girls ask me to wear the damned thing, I wear it. It's their business. Everyone else needs to tend to their own knitting and leave mine alone."

Gotcha.

"So I take this ticket to the city judge, and he asks me if I was going to plead guilty or not guilty. I say that I don't know about guilty, but I definitely wasn't wearing the damned thing that day. He asks how I'm going to pay the fine, and I tell him he'd better stick me in jail because I wasn't going to pay someone for putting his nose into other people's business."

I looked at the intake officer, both of us trying not to smile.

"So here I am."

I headed for the intake sergeant to suggest that maybe some kind of accelerated time-serving might be considered. Maybe a passing of the hat, or some such, when I passed the GenPop tank and noticed one very large, very familiar figure glaring balefully at me.

"Waldo," I said carefully, "What's on your mind?"

Waldo the Wonder Biker sneered at me and then spat off to the side.

"He was riding down Main Street wearing a chrome Nazi helmet, dark glasses, combat boots, and a smile," said the intake corporal contemplatively, "Seems there was stuff flapping in the breeze that God never intended to flap."

I grimaced, "There's not enough brain bleach in the world to fix that."

He grinned, "Gives 'tank-slap' a whole new meaning, don't it?"

"Oh, for—enough! Eww!"

I looked at Waldo, "You've been guinea-pigging the product again, haven't you?" My answer was an extremely eloquent extended middle finger.

sigh

Well, at least they got some clothes on him.

I found the intake boss, he agreed that the older gentleman didn't need to be in Durance Vile for any longer than strictly necessary, and I left to chase down the jail administrator.

Twenty minutes later, I was back with an Order of Release, scooted past the GenPop tank, and saw the older gentleman was sitting on the bench, talking softly and gesturing gently, with Waldo and two of his buddies sitting on the floor in front of the bench, listening raptly.

Huh. This was odd.

As I watched, another inhabitant of GenPop—much younger, with the ingrained sneer and bad attitude one tends to associate with some of the younger criminal element—swaggered over to the bench currently occupied by the elderly gentleman, planted himself, and drawled, "Hey, there, Old Stuff. You need to move off of my bench."

At this, Waldo raised a polite hand to the older man and said—my paw to Freyja, I heard it with my own two ears—"I'm sorry, Mr. Frank. Excuse me for just a moment."

I was looking at Waldo, seriously wondering if I should check him for a pod attachment point, when he lumbered to his feet, draped a fatherly arm across the shoulders of the youngster, and gently steered him to the bathroom area of the tank.

At this point I was seriously worried about Waldo's mental status.

Then, I hear a muted thud followed by the Waldo's dulcet tones—he'd make a fine rage metal frontman, would our Waldo—gently gargling something about eye sockets, respect, an anatomically improbable yet gruesomely fascinating version of puppeteering, and courtesy in general.

Ah. That was the Waldo I knew.

There was a final thud, and then Waldo stepped out from the bathroom area, resumed his seat on the floor in front of the bench, and said, "I'm sorry, Mr. Frank. You were saying?" And the older gentleman resumed what was obviously a riveting story.

I couldn't stand it. I beckoned, "Hey, Waldo! Come up to the bars for a moment!" Waldo's beard contorted into his usual snarl, but he got up and stomped over to talk.

I indicated the older gentleman, "What's up, Waldo? You feeling okay?"

He looked at me a moment. "Man, 'Dog, that old dude's been through some [deleted]. You can see it on his face. Really bad [deleted], but he doesn't let the [deleted] win. Dude like that earned respect."

Hell of a thing when a burned-out biker reprobate meth cook made more sense than a municipal judicial system.

Not much more that I can say to that.

FILE 29
Thing 1 and Thing 2

The joke the sheriff likes to use is that everyone else he knows has a work wife. I'm the only person he knows who has work daughters.

I tend to find that women—given an officer with draggy knuckles close by—tend to be excellent peace officers.

The majority of work done by peace officers involves communication. Women, as a whole, tend to be a lot better at communicating than the guys do.

The stories about the Things were filler I threw together one day just to have something to write on the blog, but my Gentle Readers wholeheartedly loved them. When I meet folks in the paint, they always ask me what happened to the Pink Gorilla Suit and how the Things are doing.

DD-1033 refers to the federal program that allows unused military equipment to be reutilized by civilian law enforcement agencies.

ADC is the acronym for aide de camp.

In the Army—and most probably in every other branch of the military—there is something of a tradition of miscreant E4s. The pay grade of an E4 is the first rank that involves any sort of official leadership, and, as such, is expected to make frequent faux pas. An E4 with a good head upon his shoulders, dedication to the mission and flexible scruples can often be the difference between a successful ARTEP and a "No-Go."

As a "fer instance," let us suppose that you are somewhere knee-deep in snow watching herds of brass monkeys headed south. The never-sufficiently-be-damned cab heaters on the unit's M3 Bradleys have gone Paws Up again. Your miscreant E4s will show up just before chow, having "repurposed" a "stray" trailer for some extra cab heaters.

Later on during the same exercise when you suddenly need that "stray" trailer, it will appear as long as you don't touch the bumper number. Fresh paint smears something awful.

If your E4s don't have the lion's share of the pogey-bait, the really good FMs, and the superfluous equipment that just tends to make things easier—"A shower? How in the hell did you manage to bring a pressurized shower out into the middle of BFE?!"—they know where to get their paws on it. That, along with a certain willingness to trade, bribe, beg, borrow or steal, and repurpose as required to Accomplish The Mission, tends to make the task of the military commander somewhat easier and less aneurysm-inducing. Vishnu bless 'em.

However, E4s without a mission to focus their little nefarious minds upon are often the source of the stories that begin, "This ain't no [deleted]. I took my eyes off the little [deleted]s for ten minutes, and the [Insert Descriptive Military Noun Here] exploded / burst into flame / sank / floated / wound up on eBay / got pregnant / moved, when movement was physically impossible / broke the sound barrier when not physically possible / divided by zero / wound up on top of the base watertower" are typical.

Several miles of interstate highway shut down due to tabasco-augmented smoke generators? E4s.

Nightly news video shot of hanging hams in the windows of the C-130 doing a flyby at the local airshow? E4s.

Base commander's beloved prize-winning pecan orchard mysteriously converted into high-velocity matchsticks by precise application of low-yield explosives? Bored E4s.

When I was promoted to my current position, it required thirty minutes of arguing on the part of the chief deputy before I finally accepted the promotion, and that was with the caveat that the sheriff and the chief deputy understand that I am absolutely and totally addlepated when it comes to the day-to-day administrative paperwork. "Nae problem!" sayeth them, and Thing 1 was detached to be my ADC.

Well, one year later, and I went from reporting to the head of a bureau of the sheriff's office to reporting directly to the sheriff. As such, my duties expanded considerably, and I developed another ADC: Thing 2.

Both Thing 1 and Thing 2 were sergeants with eight years+ experience in the sheriff's office. They were both literally young enough to be my children, and they were both female.

I learned several things in the last year. The first of which was that I had no idea how the fathers of daughters survive, much less maintain their sanity. Seriously. Multiple conversations in the office between those two ended with me yelping, "I'm sitting right here, and there are things that I do not need to know about!"

Secondly, when it came to flexible scruples and ruthless pragmatism, all those E4s I had known—and I'd known a lot—all those male miscreant E4s didn't hold a candle to my two female miscreant sergeants.

For example: I was sitting at my desk when Thing 1 and Thing 2 staggered through the doorway, carrying a cube-ish OD green wossname.

Me: "What is that?"

Thing 1: "It's a wossname!"

Me: "It looks like a fridge. With Air Force markings."

Thing 2: "Really?"

Me: "You've been in the DD-1033 room, haven't you?"

Thing 1: "Isn't the DD-1033 room locked?"

Me: "Yes."

Thing 2: "Then it couldn't have been the DD-1033 room. Place we found this wasn't locked."

Me: *migraine salute*

Sheriff: *wandering through with a cup of coffee* "Huh. Nice fridge. Probably fit better over by the filing cabinets."

Both Things: "Thank you, sir!"

sigh

And I wasn't known as the greatest respecter of rank around, but really....

I was wandering through the office when I heard the walrus snorting of Senior Officer Who Shall Remain Nameless in his patented Condescending Neanderthal persona, together with a voice I recognized as Thing 2. This immediately caused me to buttonhook the corner in full fire-breathing mode only to find Thing 2 apparently hanging on every word coming out of the pie-hole of SOWSRN.

SOWSRN: "Condescend. Condescend, condescend, condescendingly."

Thing 2: "Really?"

I swear I'd seen smaller eyes in anime.

SOWSRN: "Condescend!"

Behind SOWSRN, I saw Thing 1 steer a two-wheeled dolly into the open door of the office occupied, coincidentally, by SOWSRN.

Thing 2: "I never would have though of that!"

SOWSRN: "Condescending, condescend, condescended."

Thing 1 reappeared in the office doorway. Strapped to the dolly was one very large, very expensive, and thus very scarce, very *tightly controlled* widget. Thing 1, the dolly, and the widget disappeared down the hallway.

Thing 2: "It's been so very interesting talking to you! We mustn't keep you! Bye!"

SOWSRN turned and ambled back to his office, whuffing contentedly. At the door he turned. I was totally at a loss. I think I may have been covering my mouth with a hand. I'd never done that before.

Thing 2 (sotto voce while giving a small wave): "Smile and wave, boss. Smile and wave."

And then there was the time Thing 1 and Thing 2 had just unloaded a spectacular quantity of wossnames from the back end of the POV owned by Thing 2.

Me: "I really didn't think you'd be able to get all of those in there."

Thing 2: "Are you kidding? I can haul seven dead bodies AND the shovel all at the same time!"

Me: *blink*

Thing 1: *Nods happily*

Me: "What?"

Thing 2: "What?"

Sometimes it's best to just drop the conversation right there.

I swear by Freyja: Those two are going to be the death of me.

FILE 30

Definitions

After several of my shift reports wound up on the blog, I found out that jail jargon wasn't readily translatable by normal people, so I posted a quick dictionary.

LO/LOP: An abbreviation for "Lock-Off/Loss Of Privileges," which is basically disciplinary segregation. An inmate violates a rule and catches LO/LOP, we toss his butt into a solitary cell, no phone, no commissary, limited visitation, that sort of thing.

Water-checks: Inmates in a solitary cell sometimes can't—or won't—report having problems with the water faucet in the cell. Every night, an officer goes around and checks every tap in solitary to make sure that the inmate inside the cell has access to water.

SHU: Special Housing Unit. The formal term for Solitary. Sometimes also called Segregation.

Ad/SEG: Administrative SEGregation. An inmate who, for whatever reason, can't get along in General Population, but hasn't caught a case and wound up on LO/LOP. This can be due to Protective Custody, MHMR patient, Escape Risk, amongst other reasons.

TDC: Actually supposed to be TDCJ for the Texas Department of Criminal Justice. The prison system for the State of Texas. Old-time officers remember when it was called the Texas Department of Corrections.

Chain: The trip to TDC from the county. The TDC bus is the "chain bus", the trip is known as "catching chain," so on and so forth.

Jack: The handiest and most fluid word in a county inmate's vocabulary. To "jack" is to succeed against another person, either by way of guile or by physical force. For example:

"Hey, DO! Somebody jacked me for a soup!"

Translation: "Excuse me, detention officer, but person or persons unknown appear to have stolen a food item from my property locker."

"Fool! Rank 'Dog just jacked Hernandez in front of his boys!"

Translation: "Comrade! Lieutenant LawDog has caused inmate Hernandez to lose face by removing Hernandez from his Housing Area in the presence of his compatriots after Hernandez stated that he would not move!"

"Boss! I don't know, but word is that someone's gonna jack Old Con in the shower tonight."

Translation: "Officer! While neither I, nor my colleagues, are involved in any way, shape, or form, we have been given cause to suspect that another inmate—one who is younger and Less Wise in the Ways of the World—is planning to physically assault an elder in the bathing area this night."

As happens, this useful word has found its way into the lexicon of the officers.

"Hey, Sarge! 21 just jacked his beanhole."

Translation: "Sergeant, the inmate in SHU/21 is preventing officers from securing the food pass slot in the door of his cell."

Taking a shower: Alternatively, "asleep in my rack." In a Housing Area holding 24 inmates and two showers, if you drag two inmates out of the tank for a bloody fight, when you ask the other 22 inmates what happened, all 22 will invariably answer, "I don't know, boss. I was taking a shower."

I think that should cover some of the basics.

FILE 31

'Allo! 'Allo! 'Allo!

Yes, I started out an official emailed report with "'Allo! 'Allo! 'Allo!"
It was a small agency, and we could get away with stuff like that.

'Allo! 'Allo! 'Allo!

To begin with, in what has become a familiar occurrence, Inmate R was transferred out to the River from Central for housing and immediately announced that he would not be housed on West Tier.

Already knowing the answer, but being morbidly curious, we asked Inmate R who he had a problem with out that way. His answer was the name of an inmate who had been released from our custody some months back. Then, he decided that he had problems with Crips, Bloods, Latin Kings, and any other gangs he could remember. He then followed up by stating that his wife/girlfriend/spouse-like love-unit was due to have his sprog in the morning, or any day now, and he needed peace and quiet to "settle his mind."

Goodness.

He went off to SHU, where he was somewhat disturbed when it was explained to him that SHU visits were on Friday. I then gently corrected the SHU officer and stated that was true only up until his case for Disobeying a Verbal Order went to LO/LOP time, and we let him contemplate his navel for a bit.

A couple of hours later we needed a SHU cell for a suicidal inmate, so we asked Inmate R if West Tier was looking so bad now. I guess it wasn't because he's there now.

Inmate L got kited out of East/4 for unspecified problems. We put him into East/6. Two shakes of a puppy's tail later, and he was at the bars stating that he had a free-world problem with Inmate F. I asked Inmate F what sort of problem he had with Inmate L, and he apparently didn't know Inmate L from Adam's off ox. I guess that Inmate L would have problems with random inmates until he got into a tank he liked. We slung him back into East/4 anyway.

It was suicide night at the county. We were considering moving all of our suicidal inmates into one contiguous section of SHU near the officer station but didn't get around to it.

Inmate B got run out of West/2. Allegedly, West/2 thought he had snitched out their supply of nose candy. To prevent the whole "snitches get stitches" thing, we moved him to East/6.

West/8 was reading 65 degrees F, so we bumped the thermostat up a bit.

River did water checks at 0430 and shook down East/5. Trash and the usual extras found.

Intake reported nothing exciting.

Central/North did water checks at 0100; Central/Tower did them at 0220 and also shook down North/5. Again, trash and the usual.

Inmate G decided that his latest LO/LOP time meant he'd still be in SHU when he caught the chain, meaning that he'd probably do his first year of TDC in Seg. After begging most piteously to be released from Durance Vile and being refused, he decided to be a rampaging honyock. He started beating on the door, howling, yelling advice to other inmates, and has been proposing marriage as well as uninhibited trampoline sex to Thing 1 ever since.

Which, to be honest, was a little creepy to listen to.

Anyhoo, that should be about it.

I remain,

Y'r ob'd't servant,

LawDog

FILE 32

Chemistry 101

You might be surprised how often people who actually have a pretty damned good grasp of elementary chemistry have a "duh" moment and try to kill entire buildings. Yeah, I know my equations are a little off. Trust me. No one who was receiving this email knew the difference.

Good morning, ladles and germs.

On this fine early morning, let us turn our attention to chemistry. More to the point, let us meditate upon the following equation:

2NH3 + Cl2 → 2NH2Cl

Translation: Ammonia plus free chlorine released from the decomposition of NaClO (bleach) equals chloramine gas.

It's actually a much more complex equation than that, but you get the point; and while chloramine gas isn't as shagnasty as its cousin chlorine, it is somewhat more persistent.

Yes. Our Inmate Workers apparently attempted to gas Intake by pouring bleach down a drain full of ammonia.

Given the fact that at least one of the Usual Suspects involved can probably produce fourteen different varieties of Illicit Recreational Pharmaceuticals with $28 and 20 minutes of free reign inside a Circle K, yet spent several minutes staring in bumfuzzlement at the yellow-green gas drifting lazily through the kitchen says indictable things about the American Educational System... but I digress.

Sigh.

SadPanda was notified, and water was poured down said drain until the fizzing/smoking stopped—it was probably N2H4, better known as liquid hydrazine, a component of rocket fuel, by the by—and the smell went away.

Irritatedly yours, I remain:

LawDog

FILE 33

Normal Business

Yes, I referred to a lieutenant as Sad Panda. To this day, the sheriff still calls that lieutenant Panda.

To start with, Inmate W got wrapped around the axle because when he swapped his manky uniform, we gave him a 2X instead of a 3X. He proceeded to whinge at great length until I finally went to his solitary cell, listened to him, and then had him walk the catwalk in front of Officer H. Both of us felt the 2X fit just fine, so I left. Inmate W sulked.

The kitchen contractor came out here and wound up being about 20 pieces of turkey short. Sigh.

Nurse F announced that he needed to do a TB test on Inmate B in SHU/10. I practiced my diplomacy skills and then went down to SHU/10 and asked the ever-so-slightly throwed-off Inmate B if he'd like to have a TB test done. I'm here to tell you that Inmate B did not want a TB test done. Boy, howdy, did he not want one done.

I was fairly happy that I wasn't going to have to get near Inmate B with anything sharp and pointy but contacted LT SadPanda about the refusal, and that worthy ordered that Inmate B be placed in a negative-pressure cell.

Thanks to the silver tongue of Officer G, Inmate B was chained up with no problems whatsoever, but when we got to SHU/5, he decided that he didn't like me. Must have been the mustache. Anyhoo, apparently, the crazy didn't go too deep because Inmate B decided to wait on the Saying It With Saliva until the door to SHU/5 was just about all the way closed. Happily, the spit missed me by a good bit, but it kind of hurt my mustache's feelings.

East/3 had been opining about what they considered to be cold temperatures back there, but I ran a couple of temperature checks, and it ran about 72 degrees. Inmate U felt strongly enough about it that when he was pulled out for Indigent Health, he decided to open the thermostat panel and fiddle his booger-hooks around in it. I had a chat with inmate U—I may have displayed teeth—and I believed that he wouldn't be doing that again.

We shook down West/7 but found skippy-all.

Central/North stated that they had a quiet evening.

Central/Tower did the needful in West/9. Apparently, the wee lasses were stocking up on milk. And makeup.

Intake said they had "normal business." I noted, however, that Officer S had been trained on the Transport Van. I was happy to announce that he had backed into the River sally-port with no loud noises, that both the van and the doors still functioned, and that the services of the Fire Department and/or EMS were not required.

He really did need a booster seat, though.

Y'r ob'd't servant:

LawDog

FILE 34
Universal Precautions

The Chief Deputy actually opined, fairly gently, that I might be doing Bugscuffle County officers a disservice with the second and third paragraphs. Hah!

Good greetings!

To start with, Inmate B is in the hospital. When you send an officer, make sure that officer takes full universal precautions.

Officer C put his keys and phone in lockbox #1 at River, and River appeared to have tried to keep it because the key to #1 wouldn't open the lock. I went out there and tried, but I couldn't get it to open. Several officers of the knuckle-dragging persuasion offered to take a look at it, and I agreed as long as there was no hitting it with rocks, bricks, hammers, or anything else hard and heavy, no using explosives, flammable gases, or anything at high velocity, power tools were right out, and anything that might conceivably produce arterial bleeding, traumatic amputation, or loud noises in any way was strictly verboten.

Much pouting was evident, but they went out to look at it anyway. I'm pretty sure I heard the odd "Eek!" and an "Ook!"

or two, and then they came back in and handed me the entire lock... key still inside.

Sigh.

We shook down West/3 and came up with the usual string and colored smalls.

Central/North reports that Inmate G got cross-threaded with the nurse and hurt the nurse's feelings: G caught a write-up for it.

Central/South shook-down South/4, where they promptly discovered that at least five inmate workers put extra kibble in their lunch sacks and firmly caught write-ups for it.

Huh.

I remain:

LawDog

FILE 35

Orienteering

I have finally given up on the GPS battlefront. They have become so ubiquitous, and, quite frankly, so useful, that I don't mind them. Much. I still have backup maps in my pickup.

ACT ONE

The scene: A teeny-tiny office in North Texas. A map of the United States covered one wall, and LawDog was currently measuring a route betwixt Bugscuffle, Texas, and PaddlefasterIhearbanjos, NotTexas.

LawDog: "Muttermuttermutter."

Enter, stage left, Thing 2, snarfing a Cretaceous honey bun recently excavated from the depths of the office snack vending machine.

Thing 2: "Whatchadoin'?"

LawDog: "We're picking up one of our critters in some godforsaken hole in a corner of NotTexas that I've never been, so I want to have a good feel for the route. You do realize that honey buns aren't supposed to, you know, crunch?"

Thing 2 (crunching happily): "I'm young. I gotta cast-iron stomach. You do know that the sheriff bought a GPS for these trips, right?'

LawDog: "Yes, I did hear that. Weren't you using said GPS unit when you went to Tyler by way of Waco last year?"

Thing 2 (shrugging): "Nah, that was one of your fellow dinosaurs. He didn't enter the destination information properly. Garbage in, garbage out."

LawDog: "I like my maps. Look. They're even laminated."

Thing 2 (rolling eyes): "Okay, Lewis Clark, have it your way. I'll go grab the paperwork and the vehicle."

LawDog (yelping at Thing 2's retreating back): "AND Clark! Lewis AND Clark! Two different people!"

Scene closed with LawDog firmly removing the Garmin GPS unit from its Cordura case, lofting it into the open filing cabinet, and authoritatively slamming the file shut while muttering sulfurously.

ACT TWO

The scene: The interior of a standard police cruiser, some distance away from the Bugscuffle County Sheriff's Office. LawDog was in the shotgun seat, staring in disbelief as Thing 2 managed, more or less, to drive, text on a cell phone, and pound down a 64-oz Cappuccino Mongo Shake from Giblets Coffee House and Cafe all at the same time.

Thing 2 (attempting to lick the last bits of sugary caffeine goodness from the bottom of the half-gallon barrel): "Ey! Eb geb Gee Pee Ess oug!"

LawDog: "That's not a feedbag, and the last drop will do fine without you. I swear to Shiva, when your heart jumps out of your chest and starts vibrating down the road, I am not picking it up. Now what did you say, in English this time?"

Thing 2 (slightly manic grin): "Whoo, that's good stuff. Pass me the Garmin, wouldja? Hey! It's not in here!"

LawDog (piously): "Goodness. I do believe this here is a Teaching Opportunity in the Arcane Art of LandNav. Now, this here is what we call 'a map'..."

Thing 2: "Hold on. I got the GPS app for my iPhone. Give me a sec... yep... Here it is... How do you spell, 'PaddlefasterIhearbanjos'... dude, stop banging your head on the dashboard!"

Bugger!

FILE 36

Dress Code

This a Public Service Announcement that I wish would play just before docket call in every courthouse in Texas. I've been doing this for a while, and there are some things that no amount of brain bleach is going to fix.

Ladies, if I can tell from the far side of the courtroom that your G-string is tuned to A, your outfit probably violates part, or all, of the "Acceptable Court Wear" memo posted at the courtroom door by the judge.

District court is not a place to wear that cute little number that you bought for the nightclub, the beach, or any place where the major architectural features are limited to a stage and a brass pole.

And, as we have learned, just because you aren't the one on trial doesn't mean that you can't catch Contempt of Court charges.

Now we know. And knowing is half the battle.

FILE 37

The Proper Care of Handcuffs

Yes. Peace Officers have to be schooled on how to take care of their gear. And most of them won't listen. This email was featured prominently on the Patrol Bulletin Board for several years.

Ladies and gentlemen:

Let us turn our attention to the lowly, unloved handcuffs. Actually, let us turn our attention to where our handcuffs live for 98% of the time: in some form of leather, or more recently, ballistic cloth.

See that fuzzy kind of stuff lurking around in those handcuff carriers? That, my confused yet earnest apprentices, is lint. Yes, just like the stuff that breeds in your pockets.

Now, you may not know this, but when your 'cuffs are riding in the carriers, all of that lint is busily having conjugal relations with the ever-present dust, and they're doing this inside your handcuff mechanism.

I was going to say "ever-present dust-bunnies," but I've seen some of y'all's gear, and "ever-present dust buffaloes" just doesn't have the cute mental image I was going for.

Anyhoo.

Just what do you think happens to all of that mung when you squirt a jumbo-sized dose of 3-in-1 oil off into the handcuff mechanism?

Maybe nothing at first. But, as things go along, as more and more dust and lint build up, and as more oil gets coinked in there, sooner or later the inside of your handcuff mechanism is going to look remarkably like the Demon Hairball of Azgeroth exploded in there.

And sooner or later you're going to be standing there with a bemused, yet apprehensive, look on your face, a broken handcuff key in one paw, and an increasingly concerned, and still handcuffed, prisoner in the other.

Which means that someone—probably not you—is going to have to go find a set of bolt-cutters and chop your inmate loose. This will further be followed by someone else—probably with more rank than brains—in my department issuing a silly-arsed memo restricting our officers to the short, dinky, short, tiny, and altogether too-bloody-short official Smith-and-Wesson-issue key.

Ladies and gentlemen, if the official Smith-and-Wesson key was truly the bee's knees, there wouldn't be a booming business in aftermarket improved handcuff keys.

So. When you do lubricate your handcuffs, kindly use dry graphite powder or some other variety of dry, non-Demon-Hairball-forming, lubricant.

Thanks ever so.

FILE 38

A Life, Ruined

I wrote this one about thirty seconds after I got home after my shift.
This is the sort of thing that really irritates me: men who have to be
babies. Can't stand them. Oh, and he threw up the Tylenol as soon
as the Listerine hit his stomach. Honestly, sometimes I wish he hadn't,
but then I think about what a hard suicide death by Tylenol is. Eww.

You stood there, a picture of righteous indignation, and
protested that I was "ruining your life,"

Allow me to retort.

You went home to your nine-months-plus-pregnant wife at five
o'clock this morning after pub-crawling all night.

Thirty minutes after getting to bed, your offspring decided, as
is Mama Nature's prerogative, to begin the whole "Hello, World!"
thing, necessitating your wife, being the pregnant one, and all that,
waking you up with the time-honored news that it was time to go
to the hospital.

According to statements from residents of the four adjoining
apartments, your response was to bellow—and do let me quote—
"You [deleted][deleted], how could you [deleted] do this to me?!"

Seeing as how your wife was going into labor, you pretty much had to know this was coming for a least a month or two.

Anyhoo, again, according to witnesses, you followed up this wonderful display by flinging the car key out of the window of your second-floor apartment into the parking lot, where it went Goddess-only-knows-where.

While your wife tried to find the key to your family's only means of transportation to the hospital—I believe I have touched upon the whole going-into-labor bit—you went to the bathroom, where you consumed the contents of a bottle of Tylenol PM, a bottle of melatonin, a bottle of prenatal vitamins, and six Sudafed—and this is the truly heroic bit—washed them all down with half of a bottle of Listerine.

Dude... Listerine?

Apparently, being somewhat of an overachiever, you then proceeded to pound upon several doors in the apartment complex, demanding that the inhabitants thereof—and please, allow me to paraphrase—"Shoot you and put you out of your misery."

Unfortunately, no one stepped up to do society a favor, and you wound up—unventilated, damn it—back at your apartment, beating your head on the door and wailing at the top of your lungs to an uncaring Fate until your complex manager, for the sake of peace and quiet, informed you that your father-in-law had taken his Baby Girl to the hospital.

By the by, your wife's loving father tried to post your bail. Four times. Apropos of nothing, if I were you, I'd meditate on the fact that the weather in Outer Mongolia is absolutely splendid this time of year.

I'm just saying, is all.

Somehow you managed to find the car key that you had previously chucked into the parking lot and proceeded to drive your

hungover, buzzing, yet fresh-breathed self to the hospital to demand the whereabouts of your wife.

I'm sure that you were correct and that your in-laws did arrange
for your wife's admission to be kept confidential; however, the
proper way to deal with this was not to sit down on the floor in
front of the admissions desk and continually bellow your spouse's
name.

I'm guessing that you figured out all on your ownsome that
flinging yourself onto your side when hospital security arrived and
kicking your legs in a circle while shrieking at the top of your lungs
was also not a wise response.

I'd dearly like tell you that the sentence on the Security Incident
Form that read, "forcing us to deploy PepperFoam and our flash-
lights to gain compliance" didn't make me giggle like a schoolgirl,
but I'd be lying.

Snerk.

So. There you were, sniveling that if we didn't let you attend
the birth of your child, we were going to Ruin Your Life.

scratch, scratch

Old cock, I think you'd already gotten that part sewn up quite
nicely.

You'll be out of here in four hours... if you're sober by then.
Now, shut your mush and go to sleep.

Jackass.

FILE 39

Kein Engel

I should know better than to have preconceived notions about anyone else, but sometimes they sneak up on you. The officer in question retired several years later, bought a Harley Davidson with his pension checks, and is still touring the country, to the best of my knowledge.

One of the officers who worked with our department on a regular basis was in his 60s's, bald as a cue ball, grandkids out the wazoo, and about as North Texas redneck as you can get.

He drove an ancient beat-to-hell pickup with bits of hay in the bed and a Remington Model 11 in the rear window.

He carried a Smith and Wesson Combat Magnum because he didn't trust them new-fangled auto-chuckers.

His dog had a red bandanna instead of a collar.

He had every episode of *Hee-Haw* on tape.

The man was a good-ol'-boy. He was the beta version of the Standard Bubba Model.

Sometime ago back, I walked into the office, and there were a bunch of S.O. personnel giving him the hairy eyeball as he typed an incident report into the computer. He had obviously put a CD into the drive to give him music to help make the report go a little faster.

"Erst wenn die Wolken schlafengehn," growled this gentleman, happily.

I listened for a bit and then nudged another officer. "That sounds like... Rammstein," I said to her.

"Uh-huh," sayeth she, kind of big-eyed.

"Kann man uns am Himmel sehn," he graveled, head bobbing enthusiastically.

"Engel?" I guessed.

"Uh-huh."

"Wir haben Angst und sind allein," he grated, hammering away on the keyboard in time to the beat.

"He's... singing."

"Umm... Uh-huh."

"Gott weiss ich will kein Engel sein!"

Folks, that was just plain Not Right.

FILE 40

Wasabi!

While this isn't a law enforcement story per se, I thought it was close enough to include. And Peking Moon is still my favorite Chinese place in town.

———————

Some months ago I stopped off at Peking Moon for some egg flower soup and fried rice.

As I flicked open my napkin, I heard the male half of the couple in the booth across from mine say, with a large amount of relief, "They've got some [deleted] guacamole!"

This caused me to blink, and then I looked over at his plate and saw the pile of pale green paste sitting next to some of those fried egg noodles used for thickening soup.

"Self," thought I, "this here is a recipe for unpleasantness," so I said, very gently, "Excuse me, but I believe that is actually wasabi rather than guacamole."

You know, I was brought up with the understanding that offering unasked-for advice to those who were neither family nor friends just Wasn't Done.

Every once in awhile, I have been reminded of the wisdom of this.

The gentleman turned to me, and to the evident mortification of his lady, said, very softly and in a Not-From-Around-Here accent, "I don't remember asking you a goddamned thing."

Goodness.

"I especially don't need some PC, multicultural, liberal [deleted]-wipe telling me what to call something."

I propped my chin in my left hand, feigning an expression of mild interest to cover my right hand casually loosening the lid on the bottle of sriracha sauce, just in case.

"A [deleted] spade is a [deleted] spade, and I'm not going to call it a 'ding ding ching how' just because some gook handed it to me." So saying, the gentleman promptly shoveled a large amount of the green paste onto a chip, popped it into his pie hole, and chewed with emphasis.

I'd like to say that I was a big enough man that I didn't smile happily at him when he blinked, coughed, and then shot fluorescent green goo out his left nostril.

But I'd be lying.

If the old boy had a case of the hips toward "multiculturalism," one would have to wonder what the hell he was doing in a Chinese restaurant owned by a Vietnamese clan and employing Mexican cooks to serve Japanese sushi and American BBQ chicken for patrons of various European and African descents? Not to mention insulting a Maltese-American of Scottish and Mohawk ancestry?

Hell, that's practically the United Nations right there.

Ah, well.

Apparently, a nasal lavage of Japanese horseradish is not conducive to a Proper Dining Experience because the gentleman and his lady friend left about the time his vision cleared enough for him to drive.

Heh.

I was reminded of this nasty little episode because yesterday I was drifting through intake, and guess who was hanging off the bars in the detox tank slurring threats and curse words at the detention staff like an intoxicated gibbon?

Yeppers.

I probably didn't help matters much when I stopped and asked him if he'd figured out the difference between guacamole and wasabi yet.

snerk

Karma. It's a wonderful thing.

FILE 41

A Damsel in Distress

This was during the aftermath of Hurricane Katrina. We had a lot of stuff like this going on, but it seems that the climate in North Texas didn't agree with a lot of the refugees, and they scarpered off to somewhere else pretty quickly.

Gentle Readers, allow me to introduce "Joe Critter."

Joe was a fairly recent transplant to our fair city, having been forced to relocate due to Mother Nature developing a serious case of the arse regarding his former stomping grounds.

What earned Joe his moniker of "critter" was the fact that he was presently on misdemeanor probation due to his having an attitude toward romance which is generally frowned upon by society.

Now, to the best of our knowledge, Joe had managed to keep his booger-hooks to himself for a fairly admirable amount of time— probably due in no small part to Joe's erstwhile probation officer getting a wee bit put out and issuing a Violation of Probation warrant for Joe—but, it being a long summer, Joe had apparently decided he could contain himself no longer.

So Joe hopped into his late-'70s crittermobile, cruised down to a local curbside diner, pulled into a parking slot, and ordered a meal, content in the knowledge that said meal would soon be delivered by a toothsome morsel.

Now, as Joe's meal was being fixed, allow your mind's eye to fall upon the pickup truck several slots down from Joe. Witnesses became unexpectedly blank as to the description of the truck, the description of the occupants, and even the name painted on the side of the truck, but we're fairly sure that it contained several men of Hispanic extraction.

Anyhoo, back to Joe. Sure enough, Joe's munchies were delivered by a Sweet Young High School Thing, and Joe was so happy about this fact, that when she appeared at his window and greeted him, he reached forth and gathered himself a nice, big, double handful of female... umm... architecture.

Our Wee Damsel, having been gently tutored in Southern Feminine Deportment, Etiquette, and Grace by a loving Mama and Daddy, immediately stiff-armed 44 ounces of Sprite into Joe's leering mush.

Joe was somewhat taken aback by this reaction to his smoothness and responded with language that is not generally viewed as being romantic by most people. To say nothing of our Fair Maiden, who took a two-handed grip on her Serving Tray of Doom +3 and attempted to line-drive Joe's snot-locker over the scoreboard.

Now, you may be developing an inkling that Joe wasn't quite as quick on the uptake as one might hope for. He hauled off and delivered a tirade of abusive, indecent, and, yes, profane language, said language which tended to incite our Lady Fair into taking a firmer grip upon her Tray Of Doom +3 and commenced pummeling him furiously about the head and shoulders.

Sometime during the middle of this beat down, Joe's buttocks, being somewhat brighter than the rest of Joe, apparently decided that discretion was, indeed, the better part of valor, walked themselves across the bench seat, opened the passenger side door, and hopped out into the parking lot.

We know this because Joe repeatedly maintained that he was— and I quote—"A man, 'n' I don' run from no [expletive deleted] [deleted]!"

Since Joe seemed to be rather firmly attached to said buttocks, here we had Joe out in the parking lot with Our Heroine button-hooking the front of his punkmobile, battle tray at the ready.

Well, that was altogether enough for Young Joe. Steps had to be taken to preserve his reputation. And he came to his feet with a linoleum knife in one paw.

Any further action on Joe's part was interrupted by a soft voice saying, "*Perdóname, señorita.*"

Well, this kind of cleared the old tunnel vision, and Joe discovered that he and our Damsel were surrounded by a group of gentlemen, presumably out of the construction truck mentioned earlier, one of whom was 'tsk'ing his tongue at Joe whilst gently wagging an index finger.

Joe, belatedly tapping into a heretofore unused reserve of smart, froze in place.

The finger-wagger was heard to murmur, "*¿Con su permiso?*" before a very large gentleman, with a huge mustache over a bigger grin, firmly relieved Joe of his pig-sticker. Then, witnesses affirm that the gentlemen grinned at our Sweet Young Thing, made "get-on-with-it" gestures, and went back to noshing on fries and Cokes while still surrounding the combatants.

Ahem.

Since this is Texas, let us say that our Damsel then "held the suspect for questioning by police."

Yes, that did nicely. The suspect was, indeed, still present when police arrived. Followed by the ambulance.

Responding officers noted that there may have been some quite understandable enthusiasm expressed in said "holding for police."

Heh.

FILE 42
Your Wife

*More often than not Domestic Violence arrestees try to justify their
actions to anyone who'll listen. Usually, that's the intake personnel,
who not only don't care, but don't want to be dragged into court
because the arrestee inadvertently confessed during the justification.
I have never said this to Domestic Violence arrestees. That's what my
blog is for.*

Dear Mr. Critter,

I have listened patiently to your tale of woe and your explanations as to "what really happened," and I have heard your attempts
to justify your actions three times in a row.

I still don't believe you.

No, you have had your say. Now it is my turn.

You and your wife divorced 19 months ago. A year and a half—
almost two years past—your wife stopped being your wife.

You have explained the 500-plus phone calls over the last month
as concern for your children. I can understand paternal concern.

You have explained sitting in your parked car across the street from your ex-wife's house as loneliness for the children of whom you have lost custody. I understand loneliness.

You have explained following your ex-wife from a restaurant to her home before blocking her car in the driveway and calling the police as merely a father's concern for his children being un-seat-belted in a moving vehicle. I understand concern for your children.

However, I have listened to your explanations, and I have listened to your two free phone calls during the booking process, and I am, by nature and by training, an observant man.

Do you realize that while you have mentioned your ex-wife multiple times, in not one single instance have you used her name?

Not only this, but you continually refer to the woman who divorced you nineteen months ago as "My Wife."

Not "My Ex-Wife." Not "That [deleted]" or even the ever-popular "That [deleted]ing [deleted]."

No. You repeatedly say such things as, "I followed My Wife from the eatery because…"; "They were in My Wife's house…"; "My Wife doesn't take care…"; "My Wife doesn't realize…"

The thing is, she stopped being your wife nineteen months ago. You've had more than enough time for that little fact to sink in.

That unconscious possessiveness tells me all that I need to know.

The warrant you were arrested on is for felony stalking. There is a petition for an Order for Emergency Protection heading for the magistrate's desk, and it will be served before your release from custody sometime tomorrow.

I suggest you use the time between now and then to contemplate and to indulge in some deep-breathing exercises; you could meditate on the thousands of other fish in the sea… that sort of thing.

Of course, you might also consider reaching down, taking a firm grip on both ears, and tugging until you see daylight, but that's up to you.

Nothing but love,

LawDog

FILE 43

Canis Interruptus

This was not a Harry Potter spell, but rather, a timely Phrase of the Day

---

You had been chasing a critter through multiple backyard. He was half your age and not encumbered by the forty pounds of bat-belt and armor required by Modern Policing; therefore he was actually picking up speed as he anteloped over fence after fence after fence.

As you were leaning against a tree, wheezing and swearing that you were going to start going to the gym tomorrow, he cleared the next-to-last fence... accompanied by the sudden joyous baritone barking that could only come from the throat of a dog the size of a Tyrannosaurus Rex.

This is technically referred to as *canis interruptus*, and it engendered a warm-and-fuzzy feeling in your chest and a jaunty whistle to your lips as you strolled happily down the alley to the heartrending sounds of shrieking, tearing, crashing, and general doggy mayhem.

FILE 44

Buster and the Black Belt

*You'll notice that this is actually two stories in one. The kid in the
first story has gone on to a munificent career as a lousy criminal. The
dog is the second one is still wearing his bandanna proudly, but, to
the best of my knowledge, hasn't whacked any chickens since then. I'm
sure that if he had, his proud dog daddy would have let me know.*

0900 hours:

I was informed that my presence was requested at Bugscuffle
County Justice Court, Precinct 1/2. I parked my cruiser outside
the TruValue hardware store in the spot marked by the sign that
reads "Thou Shalt Not Park Here," wended my way past the nail
bins, tossed a cheery wave to Jimmy Don, and scooted up the stairs
to the second-floor courtroom.

The sound of a badly mangled version of a Hank Williams,
Junior song lustily warbled at the top of someone's lungs was the
first clue I had that things Might Be Interesting.

"Godda shot-rifle, a sumthin' 'n' a four-drive wheel!"

I tapped gently on the frosted-glass panel of the door and
opened it to find the judge at his desk, elbow planted firmly, and

chin cradled in hand as he gazed in mild bemusement at what I guess was the defendant.

Unless it was the guy sitting next to the singer, face cradled in both hands, but I was betting he was the lawyer.

"Ah can skin a trot, 'n' run a buck-line!"

I cocked an eyebrow at the judge, "I hate it when I skin a trot." The judge snorted, there was a muffled groan from the lawyer, and the court reporter giggled. I grinned and sneaked a look at her legs before opining, "I'm guessing the defendant—"

Never taking his chin off his palm or his gaze off of Breakfast Theater, the judge whisked a sheet of paper off the desk and handed it to me. It was an Adjudication of Guilt for Public Intoxication and a Commitment Order for five days. It was, I further noted, on a PI ticket the sheriff had written two weeks ago.

"Ah," sayeth I, "And the subject would be—"

"Drunker than a waltzing pissant" opined the judge.

"Not to mention—"

"All of nineteen years old."

"And it's only—"

"Nine-thirty in the morning."

"Goodness. Should I cite him for Minor in Consumption or Public Intoxication on the way to the pokey?"

The subject in question promptly, albeit shakily, climbed on top of the table and defiantly bellowed, "CUZ A CUNK-, CONN-, CONNTREE BOY CAN SHUR-, SHUR, SOME-THIN', DAMMIT!"

The judge pondered this performance for a moment. "Yes."

And we were off.

1115 hours:

Met with Reporting Party concerning a Dangerous Dog.

I pulled into a small trailer park at 1777 Ranch-to-Market Road. I had the distinct feeling that the man waving the baby parka at me was most probably going to be the Reporting Party.

Upon closer inspection, the baby parka turned out to be an extremely deceased chicken. The owner of the decedent had no doubts as to the cause and perpetrator of the vile deed.

"Vicious! Brutal! Da-angerous! I want that hound locked up or put down. And somebody's gotta pay!" He was extremely wrought-up, and to avoid getting smacked with a dead chicken, I gently removed the carcass from his grip.

"So," I asked, frowning as I noticed the scar tissue from where the rooster's comb had been removed quite some time ago, "Are you sure it's the dog next door?"

"Sure?! Am I sure?! I saw the mutt run into my yard and maul my five-hundred-dollar prize rooster! Who's going to pay me for my rooster, huh?! Who?"

I raised my hand—the one not currently occupied with a chicken corpse—in a "peace" gesture. "Let me go talk to your neighbor." Without waiting for a reply, I walked to the trailer next door, pausing to look over the back fence belonging to the bereaved chicken owner.

Five other roosters looked back at me. All were missing their combs, and all were on six-foot lengths of chain that prevented them from touching one another.

Oh-ho, thought I.

I knocked on the door of the trailer occupied by the owner of the rampaging mongrel.

It opened, and I was faced with a very large man, gray hair escaping from under a gimme cap, full gray beard and mustache braided with tiny pewter skulls, black leather vest and knuckle rings on every finger, all of which were displaying skulls, bones, and various incarnations of death worked in pewter.

Oh. Joy.

"Morning, sir. I'm Deputy LawDog, Bugscuffle S.O. and there seems to have been an incident with your dog."

I peered around the old boy, fully expecting to see a Rottweiler or a Pit Bull, but he interrupted my looking around with a slightly abashed confession.

"It's my fault, really. That damn rooster got up on the yard gnome and started crowing like to beat anything you ever heard. I went to the door and yelled at it to git, and Buster, well, Buster heard me yellin' and kind of took off and jumped."

"All right then. Before we go any further, sir, where is Buster? I'd hate for there to be some kind of misunderstanding while I'm talking to you."

I suddenly realized that the man had a chihuahua draped across his forearm. Granted, it had a tiny black bandanna with white skulls around its neck, but it was still a chihuahua. Then, I noticed the Spongebob Squarepants band-aid sliding down its furry foreleg. And fresh blood under the band-aid.

You've got to be... I pointed at the little creature, "Buster?"

Buster wagged his tail happily at me.

"Yes, sir, this is my Buster."

I looked at the dog. He rolled over on the man's arm to have his belly scritched. I lifted the chicken. Seven pounds. Easily. I looked at Buster. Not seven pounds. If you stuffed his bandanna with bricks, five or six pounds. Maybe.

"Now I know that Buster shouldn't'a done killed that chicken. But it was in his yard, and Buster gets kind of territorial, and he kind'a gets mad at the things I get mad at. But I done offered that man a hundred bucks for his chicken even though it was in my yard where it had no right to be!"

I held up a hand and looked at the chicken-slaughtering brute, kicking his back leg in an orgy of bliss as his tummy got scratched. I walked over to the garden gnome. It was well within the property limits. Blood and feathers everywhere.

I left the man with his vicious killer and returned to the chicken owner.

"That's a five-hundred-dollar prize-winning rooster there!"

I held up a hand, forestalling the impassioned speech that was clearly building up steam.

"You're about to lie to me. Again. And that would be unwise."

He looked at me, bottom lip quivering.

"Take the hundred dollars. I found where—let me speak! I found where the chicken was killed. It's not even close to your property. You don't want his dog to kill your chickens, keep them off his property. Now, you can insist that I investigate and file a report. If I do so, anything I find during my investigation will be acted upon. As a creative articulation, let's say that I find that someone around here is raising gamecocks for fighting. Well, then, I'd have to act on that. And serving search warrants and seizing everything someone owns because he's involved in a criminal enterprise... well, that just causes heartburn all the way around."

He looked at me.

I smiled.

"Sir," he licked dry lips, "Come to think, a hundred bucks for that chicken is almighty reasonable."

I handed him his dead chicken. "I'll just go deliver the news then."

Buster's owner took the news with some relief. I looked at the chihuahua, dozing happily on the man's arm.

"He doesn't weigh as much as the rooster did."

"No, sir, that he don't."

"That rooster had a black belt in chicken-fu."

"Yes, sir, I reckon he would have to have."

We looked at Buster. A slow, proud smile escaped the beard and creeped across the man's face.

"He sure [deleted] that chicken up, didn't he?"

sigh

Does anyone else have days like this?

FILE 45

The Pink Gorilla Suit

When "LawDog" is mentioned in some parts of the Internet, this is what comes to mind. Yes, this is the Infamous Pink Gorilla Suit Story. It's been reposted in a lot of other places, and I've even been cajoled into performing it live a time or two.

It is easily the most popular story I ever wrote on my blog, and it almost never got completed.

I had written the first half right up to the part about "Dirty Deeds Done Dirt Cheap", and then I had an episode of Writer's Block that lasted several years.

When I say "Writer's Block", I had no problem writing other stuff. But the first half was written before I had a blog, and a lot of my other stories were written while the second half was still percolating.

Weird.

The most common question I get is something along the lines of: Where is the Pink Gorilla Suit now?"

Hah!

A big part of the sheriff's "Work smarter, not harder" philosophy involved the fine art of misdirection. If a subject was so confused that he wasn't perzackly sure which way was up, then he probably wouldn't be causing the sorts of problems which require extra paperwork. Or ER trips. Depositions. Lawsuits. That kind of thing.

Which brings us to the Pink Gorilla Suit.

sigh

Tucked not-far-enough in the back of the evidence closet was a costume that the S.O. had picked up from somewhere. As the name suggests, this was a gorilla costume, mostly pink.

Now, when I say pink, I don't think y'all quite understand the depth of pinkness we are contemplating here: It was pink-pink. Neon pink. Fluorescent pink. A pink not found anywhere in nature. A pink that, in and of itself, constituted a radiation hazard. A shade of pink which, after a single glimpse, would cause even the most flamboyant Mardi Gras costumer to protest that things had gone too, too far.

Pink.

Now, bad as this mental picture is, the insane designer of this suit had apparently decided long ago that having only one eye-searing shade was simply too boring, so this poor unfortunate had added spats, gloves, cuffs, a bow tie, and a top hat.

All very natty, and all very mauve.

We will now pause to give the Gentle Reader enough time to fully digest the Sheer Awfulness that was the Pink Gorilla Suit.

Yeah.

Anyhoo, we had gotten a search warrant. Apparently, our Usual Suspects had graduated to Methamphetamine, Distribution Of and had stashed a functioning meth lab inside a garage apartment out behind the house of, and belonging to, the grandparents of Usual Suspect #3.

Our pre-warrant briefing consisted of the sheriff reminding us of some of the knottier problems associated with executing a search warrant on a meth lab, most of which seem to involve the uncontrolled high-speed random disassembly of various items and/or people, and finishing off with a reminder that the Standard Obscenity Procedure for this sort of thing was to distract the critters long enough for officers to secure the scene without any of what the sheriff referred to as "fuss and bother."

That's when the chief deputy handed me the box containing the Pink Gorilla Suit.

sigh

There I was, sulking down the street in front of God and everybody, wearing a neon pink gorilla suit with mauve accouterments over jeans, armor, and a pistol, with a search warrant tucked securely in my sleeve, and the sheriff's exhortations to "Be Distracting" ringing in my ears.

Bearing in mind that the search warrant was only for the garage and apartment and not wanting to find myself in Animal Control's bad graces again, I moped up the steps to the main house and rang the doorbell.

Light footsteps approached the door and were followed by a long pause. Then, I heard the sound of the footsteps heading away from the door.

sigh

I pulled my badge out from the collar of the suit and held it prominently in one paw.

This time the footsteps were accompanied by a heavier tread. I waved my badge at the peephole and was rewarded with the door opened just enough for me to be beheld by an extremely suspicious eye.

I tipped my hat (top, mauve) politely, "Afternoon, sir. Sheriff's office. Pardon the interruption, but we're going to be serving a warrant on your garage and apartment. The sheriff told me to tell you that he'd take it kindly if y'all would stay inside the house until we have things under control."

Long pause.

"Under control," murmured the gentleman slowly as he opened the door a little more fully. "Are you planning on that there control thing happening any time soon?"

Smart aleck.

"Can't really tell with this kind of thing, sir. We'll let you know as soon as possible."

I figured I might as well get this over with. I leaned slightly right and looked around the gentleman to the lady of the house. "Ma'am," tip of the hat again, "Mind if I borrow some of your flowers?"

She looked at me, at the innocent tulips on the edge of the walk, and back to me.

"Umm. Go right ahead. You do know that you're pink?"

"Hadn't noticed, ma'am" I lied gallantly while selecting a pair of yellow tulips that set off my mauve spats nicely, "We'll be around back if you need us."

I trudged back to the street, turned left, and walked down to where the driveway from the garage entered the street. The garage sat about twenty feet or so back, with the apartment being the second floor of the structure.

The only ways in or out were two roll-up garage doors and a people-type door facing me, and the only windows to be seen were on the side facing the street.

sigh

Distracting. Hah.

I looked around and made sure that I was at the junction of the driveway and the public street, set my top hat securely on the mask, straightened the gloves and spats, took a deep breath... and burst into a full-blown, top-of-the-lungs, you'll-bloody-well-hear-this-one-at-Carnegie-Hall rendition of *Dirty Deeds Done Dirt Cheap*. While using the tulips as the microphone.

By God.

snort, snort

I did the works. Vocals. Backup vocals. Sound effects. Kinda-sorta instruments. Howling. The whole nine yards.

And, of course, *Dirty Deeds* has that lovely guitar solo, which lends itself quite nicely to an air guitar—excuse me—*tulip* guitar performance.

Well, if it didn't, it does now.

Unfortunately, the tulip guitar solo naturally kind of led into a dance.

It was a fairly energetic dance. And maybe a touch expressive.

All right! I'll admit it. There was an amount of gyrating going on.

However, I do not think that I was doing, quote *"The gorilla version of a fan dance,"* unquote. I don't think that you can do, quote *"Suggestive things with a hat,"* unquote, when you're wearing a fur suit, and that over jeans, and I do take umbrage at the suggestion that I, quote *"Gave them the 'Full Monkey,'"* unquote.

Anyhoo, I dug down deeeeeep for that final, "YEARGH!" clutched my tulips to my chest with both paws, and slowly, dramatically, and with the greatest amount of majesty that can be summoned while wearing a gorilla suit, fell over backward onto the gentle grass.

Hell of a performance, if I do say so myself.

So, I lay there, pondering the blameless sky and trying to remember if, at any time during the Academy, any of my instructors had ever mentioned the words "Pink," "Gorilla," and "Suit" in the same day, much less the same sentence, when over my natty, mauve spat-adorned toes, I noticed some faces in the window panel of the garage door.

I was beginning to wonder if maybe my performance was a little too good when the door opened and the Usual Suspects slipped out to stand just shy of my fuchsia carcass.

Usual Suspect #1: "Dudedudedude, umm, dude, umm, wow."

Usual Suspect #2: "Umm... it's... umm..."

Usual Suspect #1: "Dude, this is, like, not good, okay? Not good, dude. You can't stay here, okay?"

Usual Suspect #2: "Umm... it's... ummm..."

Pink, I think to myself, pink. The word you're looking for is pink.

Usual Suspect #1: "Dude! Top hat! It's not an it. It's a he! See the hat?"

At this point, Usual Suspect #3—the only female in the group—stopped gnawing on her thumbnail long enough to vibrate out, "Chickswearhats. Youlikemyhat!"

Usual Suspect #2: "Furry! He's... ummm... furry?"

Geez. Behind the group, I saw the sheriff, hands in pockets, grass stem between his teeth, stroll nonchalantly into the structure through the door the Usual Suspects had left open. Right behind him, grinning at me, went the chief deputy.

Usual Suspect #1 glared at #2: "Dude, he can't help the way he was born. Dude!"

Usual Suspect #2: "Umm… pink. And pink."

Ah-hah! Thought I.

Usual Suspect #1: "Dude, Pinky. Come on, Pinky. Dude, you can't stay here, dude. Oreos! Pinky, dude, oreos in the kitchen, man. Oreos! Let's go get the oreos!"

So saying, #1, and after a short pause, #2 began lifting me up, and as they got their shoulders under my arms, I saw the sheriff pop out of the garage and give me a thumbs up.

About bloody time.

I reached into my left sleeve, pulled out the folded paper, handed it to Usual Suspect #1, and announced, quite firmly, "Sheriff's office, search warrant."

Usual Suspect #1 stared at me, and then his eyes welled up with tears, "Dude, dude, ah man. Dude! We're buds, dude!" #2 pivoted slowly and began to oh-so-innocently wander away, only to be corralled and cuffed by the grinning night deputy.

"No, no, dude," offered #1 as I cuffed him, "No! This ain't right, man! You sold out, dude! That's so wrong!"

I turned him around, reached up, pulled that damned gorilla mask off, dropped it on the ground, and shook a hot pink finger in his face, "Listen to me."

All three sets of jaws dropped.

"Are you listening? Quit guinea-pigging the product. Seriously."

I was pretty sure that I wasted my breath, given the completely bumfuzzled expression on the face of #1 as he looked from the discarded mask to me and back again; and #2 was just staring at me with his face scrunched up like a monkey doing a math problem.

And then the magnitude of the sheer depravity that local law enforcement was capable of hit Usual Suspect #3.

"OhmyGawdohmyGawdohmyGawd," she gasped, bouncing up-and-down like a demented jack-in-the-box. "Nonono, youdo-nunnerstand, nonono!" She took a deep breath, her expression one commonly seen upon the countenance of saints who have just beheld the vilest depths of the utter darkness of the human soul.

"THEY."

"SKINNED."

"PINKY!"

The chief deputy was immediately seized by a coughing fit; the sheriff seemed to find something intensely fascinating in the overhead cloud cover whilst rubbing his mustache ferociously; Usual Suspect #1 let out a soul-rending shriek as he fell to his knees, sobbing and nuzzling the discarded gorilla mask, and #3 hurled imprecations and threats in my general direction.

I looked at my fellow peace officers, all finding this to be incredibly funny, gathered my tattered pride and dignity, straightened the bow tie and spats, extracted my hot pink gorilla mask from #1, tucked it under my arm, announced firmly, "I'm going home, now," turned, and began marching down the street.

But not before the night deputy slid a comradely arm about my shoulders and said, with steely sympathy, "I know it doesn't feel like this now, but your betrayal was for their own good. Go home. Drown your sorrows in oreos. Things will be better in the morning."

Oh, you're a right bastard, you are.